Methods in Teaching
Basic Business Subjects

FOURTH EDITION

Methods in Teaching
Basic Business Subjects

Donald Lee Musselman

James Madison University
Harrisonburg, Virginia

Vernon A. Musselman

Professor Emeritus
University of Kentucky
Lexington, Kentucky

Kawanna J. Simpson

University of Kentucky
Lexington, Kentucky

The Interstate
Printers & Publishers, Inc.

Danville, Illinois 61832

METHODS IN TEACHING BASIC BUSINESS SUB-JECTS, Fourth Edition. Copyright © 1980 by The Interstate Printers & Publishers, Inc. All rights reserved. Prior editions: 1967, 1971, and 1975. Printed in the United States of America.

Library of Congress Catalog Card No. 79-91179

ISBN 0-8134-2107-1

Preface

The classroom procedures utilized in teaching the basic business subjects are considerably different from those employed in teaching the skill subjects. More variety is needed, and socialization, discussion, and problem solving come to the forefront. This book contains many examples, illustrations, and techniques adapted from actual classroom observations and experiences of dozens of successful teachers.

The authors are indebted to colleagues and former students who furnished the encouragement, inspiration, incentive, and assistance needed to bring this work to fruition.

The art sketches were prepared by Raymond Gilmore and Tom Vantreese, College of Education, University of Kentucky. Our special thanks to them for their excellent work. It is hoped that this book will prove to be valuable to teachers and education students who are seeking help in the teaching of general business, business law, economics, and consumer economics.

Donald Lee Musselman
Vernon A. Musselman
Kawanna J. Simpson

Lexington, Kentucky

Table of Contents

CHAPTER 1

Basic Business Subjects
in the Curriculum

The Policies Commission for Business and Economic Education issued these statements in 1961 and reissued them in 1970:

> Business education is an effective program of occupational instruction for secondary students desiring careers in business.
>
> Business education has an important contribution to make to the economic literacy of all secondary school students.
>
> Business education is desirable for students who plan programs requiring post-secondary and higher education in the field of business.[1]

The literature in professional business education periodicals affirms repeatedly these dual objectives of business education. The attainment of economic literacy on the part of secondary school youth is clearly the responsibility of the business education teachers.

Regardless of how a person earns a living, he experiences many contacts with business activities. Every individual wants

---

[1]Floyd and Doris Crank, "Historical Perspectives of Education for Business," NBEA Yearbook, 1977, p. 7.

to receive maximum return on money saved or invested. Every person is interested in financial planning for both spending and saving. It is this area of business knowledge needed by everyone that is called basic business. Everyone needs to know about the services offered by commercial banks. How does one compare the relative costs of owning or renting a home? How much insurance is enough, and what kinds of coverage are best? What does credit cost and where can it be obtained? When must a contract be in written form? These are but a few of the areas of business know-how everyone needs. The courses which are normally offered at the high school level, and are considered to be basic business subjects, are general business, business law, principles of economics, and consumer economics.

EDUCATION

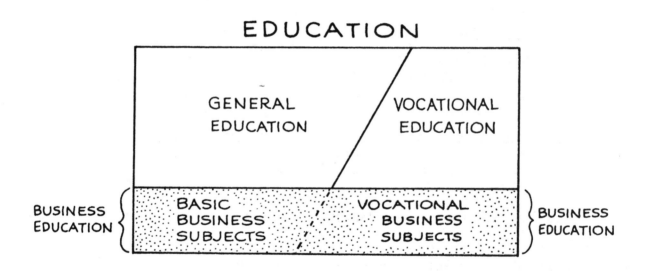

The accompanying diagram depicts the dual role of business education--general knowledge and specific occupational study. This book is concerned with the first--general business education.

COURSE CONTENT

A basic business task force in California suggests that the following areas be stressed in general business:

The Business System
    You and the business economy
    Characteristics of a free enterprise
        system

Career Education--Planning Your Future

Consumer Education
    Consumer buying
    Services for consumers
    Problems of the consumer
    Sources of consumer information

Credit
    Establishing credit
    Cost of using credit

Citizenship Responsibilities

Insurance

Money
    Borrowing money
    Planning a savings program
    Planning the use of your income[2]

In a business law class, the major units are:

The Judicial System
Contracts
Property Including Bailments
Principal-Agent Relationships
Wills and Estates
Negotiable Instruments
Employer-Employee Relationships

The major units of study to be included in a consumer economics class are:

_____

[2]Eileen B. Gentry, "Evaluating Instructional Objectives in Basic Business and Economics," NBEA Yearbook, 1978, p. 226.

Financial Planning--Budgeting and Record
  Keeping
Buymanship
        Planning and scheduling
        Cash buying vs. credit buying
        Instalment purchases
        Seasonal sales
        Consumer information
        Information on labels

In the area of economics, the Joint Council on Economic Education has recommended that courses include the following topics:

        Economic Scarcity
        Factors of Production
        Supply and Demand
        Money and Credit
        Business Cycles
        The Role of Government
        Comparative Economic Systems
        Saving Investment and Capital[3]

There is some overlapping in the subject matter commonly taught in economics, consumer economics, and general business. At the same time, the courses in each of these areas include some topics not taught in the others. This is shown rather clearly by the following outlines.

MAJOR COMMON ELEMENTS OF CONTENT

General Business, Consumer Economics, High School Economics

    1. American Economic System
    2. Credit
    3. Labor-Management Relations
    4. Money and Banking
    5. Savings and Investments

---

[3]Ibid.

4

General Business and Consumer Economics

1. Buymanship
2. Insurance
3. Money Management

General Business and High School Economics

1. Governmental Economic Planning
2. Personal Economic Planning
3. Organization of Business

Consumer Economics and High School Economics

1. Consumer and the Economy
2. International Economics
3. Taxation

MAJOR SEPARATE ELEMENTS OF CONTENT

General Business

1. Personal Records Management
2. Travel, Transportation, Communication
3. Citizenship Responsibilities

Consumer Economics

1. Investing in a Home
2. Consumer and the Law
3. Consumer Protection--Government and Private Sources
4. Advertising and the Consumer
5. Investing in Oneself

High School Economics

1. Economic Resources
2. Productivity and Technological Change
3. Operation of a Market System
4. Problems of Income Distribution
5. Profits and Wages
6. Measuring Economic Performance
7. Spending Behavior and Causes of Instability
8. Economic Security and Welfare Programs
9. Agriculture
10. Urban Economic Problems
11. Problems of Underdeveloped Nations
12. Comparative Economic Systems
13. Economic History

COURSE OBJECTIVES

Desirable outcomes of socio-business economic education involve proper attitudes towards business and society; the development of concepts and understandings; the ability to analyze facts and situations in order to reach conclusions; the making of decisions; and an understanding of the business environment in which one lives and works.

General Business

The primary aim of general business is to develop economic understanding. In teaching this course, one should emphasize the fundamental economic principles that characterize a capitalistic economic system. It aims at building sound economic citizenship-- the individual's role as a producer, wage earner, and citizen. The student learns how his votes in the marketplace have a bearing upon economic policy formation and decision making. The secondary aim of general business is to develop wise consumer- ship--expertise in using the goods and services supplied by our business system.

Economics

The chief aim of a course in economics is quite similar to that of a course in general business. In economics, however, the students go into economic theory and principles to a much deeper and broader degree. Also, since the students are older, the content material is on a higher level.

Consumer Economics

The chief objectives of consumer economics are similar to the secondary aim of general business--wise money management, including budgeting, record keeping, saving, and investing, and wise buymanship. As is true for the students in economics, the students who study consumer economics are juniors and seniors in high school; thus, the material in this course is presented on a higher level than the material in general business.

Business Law

The course in business law does not attempt to prepare a student to serve as his own attorney. Quite to the contrary, it aims at helping him know when he needs to consult an attorney. Its function is to help the student become familiar with those legal principles with which he comes in contact in everyday living. An acceptable list of objectives for students enrolled in a class in business law is given here:

1. To learn about the system of jurisprudence as administered by the state and national courts.
2. To develop a respect for law and order and constituted legal authority.
3. To become familiar with those basic principles of law that are especially significant in business.

4. To learn about important basic legal forms one might use that do not require the assistance of an attorney.

5. To know when it is prudent to consult an attorney.

6. To learn how best to cooperate with legal authorities for the benefit of society and for the rendering of justice to all.

When considering the basic business areas as a whole, one could very well state as desirable outcomes the following list, as suggested by W. Harmon Wilson in the <u>Eastern Business Teachers Yearbook</u>, "Social-Business Economic Education," Volume XLI. Though published several years ago, this list applies aptly to today.

1. The development of a sufficient vocabulary to understand the subject under consideration.

2. The acquisition of sufficient facts to be realistic and to serve as a basis for reaching desirable goals.

3. A knowledge of procedures and practices in business and society in order to understand the framework in which decisions must be made and economic services are performed.

4. An understanding of institutions of business and society in order to understand their functions and their services.

5. The development of basic sets of principles by inductive or deductive reasoning.

6. The development of concepts.

7. The ability to solve problems, including mathematical problems, and to arrive at decisions.

8. The ability to distinguish facts from opinions.

9. The ability to analyze controversial and opposing points of view and to arrive at decisions.

TEACHING METHOD

There are essential differences in the nature of basic
business subjects and vocational business subjects and the
ways in which they are taught. Vocational business subjects
emphasize a uniform lesson plan, skill building procedures, laboratory activities, and a strong, rather inflexible, reliance
upon the textbook. In contrast, basic business subjects emphasize variety in the lesson plan, socialization activities
(class discussions, research projects, reports), individual and
group projects, and wide use of current materials to supplement
the textbook. Teachers who understand these differences and plan
accordingly succeed at, and enjoy, teaching the basic business
subjects.

Variety in Lesson Planning. Basic business subjects
offer many opportunities for varying one's classroom teaching
pattern. In the first place there are many different ways one
can begin the class--by telling a story, asking a question, using
a pretest, or posing a case problem, to name only a few.[4]

Every teacher has his favorite teaching method, but in basic
business classes one can use all methods--class discussion, lecture, supervised study, oral and written reports, or problem
solving.[5] Successful teachers of basic business subjects use
them all, and this variety enhances student learning.

Just as there are many ways to introduce a new topic, and a
variety of teaching procedures to employ, basic business subjects
lend themselves to a variety of review techniques. Review exercises can be clothed in game-type procedures, such as tic-tac-toe,

---

[4]Each of these, and others, is discussed in Chapters 3
and 6.

[5]These teaching procedures are discussed individually in
Chapter 9.

or matching games, or in athletic contests, such as football, basketball, or baseball, at the different seasons of the year.[6]

Socialization Activities. That group of subjects now commonly called basic business subjects was once referred to as social business subjects. In fact, every teaching device employed by good social studies teachers may be used when teaching basic business subjects. Among the favorite devices commonly employed are socialized recitations, committee activities, buzz sessions, and group projects. These activities encourage the give-and-take that occurs when a student is a member of a small group of his peers. It provides him an opportunity to contribute to and profit from membership in a group in which he is accepted as a worthy member. It is when a person is a member of a small group that he exerts his greatest influence and in turn is influenced most by others.

Individual and Group Research. Assignments vary in basic business classes. Every student doesn't do exactly what all others do. In fact, not only do assignments vary from one student to another, but also each individual may decide the specific things he will do. Teachers may offer a suggested list of projects from which the students may choose, or sometimes the students themselves propose activities for the teacher's approval. In many instances guidelines are given and the students work within them.

Individual and group projects help students develop the ability to accept and fulfill responsibilities and provide them the opportunity to use their initiative and creativity. Most students learn more from research study than from studying the textbook. Furthermore, what they learn in this manner provides a challenge and satisfaction not normally attained from reading the text. When doing research projects, the students read widely and in depth, exploring all facets of a given topic. In most

---

[6]These are all discussed more fully in Chapter 10.

cases their end products are either oral reports presented to the class or written reports submitted to the teacher.

The utilization of individual and small group research projects is one approach toward maximum development of each student's ability to perceive, understand, and remember. It helps to develop each student's individual talents. It illustrates one method of putting into practice the idea expressed by the Chinese proverb: "What I hear, I forget; what I see, I remember; what I do, I understand."

Current Supplementary Materials. The textbook constitutes the common body of knowledge possessed by teacher and students. Newspapers, periodicals, company bulletins, booklets, and pamphlets provide enrichment data to supplement the textbook information. U.S. News & World Report, Changing Times, and Business Week are especially helpful.

Periodic reports on current events in the business world provide both the framework and the incentive for reading and browsing through these magazines regularly. The individual and group projects discussed earlier achieve the same objectives. Current materials supply the "spice" for most of the topics studied in the basic business subjects.

CORRECT GRADE PLACEMENT FOR BASIC BUSINESS COURSES

A textbook can be written at only one reading level. If a book is written for use by juniors and seniors, it will be too difficult for most freshmen and sophomores. Therefore, it is important that basic business courses be offered at the correct grade levels. The grade levels usually recommended for them are:

Course	Grade Levels
General Business	9th and 10th
Business Economics	11th and 12th
Consumer Economics	11th and 12th
Business Law	11th and 12th

Another important consideration in correct grade placement is to enroll students of the same levels in the same classes. For example, if general business is offered to tenth-, eleventh-, and twelfth-grade students, some sections may be open to those in the tenth and eleventh grades only, while other sections may be open only to juniors and seniors. When general business is offered in both junior and senior high school, two different books should be adopted so as to have books which are written at different levels of difficulty.

THE STUDY ABILITIES OF STUDENTS

Teachers should not assume that their students have mastered the basic study skills needed to succeed in their classes. Studies of the reading ability of tenth graders show that they vary over a range of six grades in their ability to read, when measured according to vocabulary and comprehension. They do not know how to read their textbooks and pick out key ideas and summary sentences. Many of them have not established regular places and times for studying, and they neither follow any systematic plan for review, nor appreciate its importance and value.

One of the first steps in helping these students develop their study abilities is to demonstrate for them the correct way to study a textbook. This may be done by turning through one of the early chapters in the book and showing them how to search out answers to the questions asked or suggested by the headings and subheadings in the book. Their attention should also be called to the new vocabulary terms which usually appear in italics or boldface type. They should be shown that the review questions at the end of the chapter are helpful in checking on their mastery of the text material. A suggested study procedure in outline form follows. It would be helpful for the teacher to duplicate this and give each student a copy after demonstrating its use.

How to Study Your Textbook

1. Survey the chapter to see what it is about. What are the main subtopics?

2. Read the chapter through.

    a. What questions are asked or suggested by the boldface headings? Find the answers to these questions.

    b. Underscore key words and summary sentences.*

    c. Write important ideas and questions in the margins.*

    d. After reading a main section, ask yourself what is said mainly.

    e. Outline the chapter--this shows relationships: What points are more important and what points are less important than others?

    f. Ask yourself these questions:

        (1) What does it say?
        (2) What do I not understand?
        (3) What is most important? Why?
        (4) Can I explain it?

3. Study the review questions at the end of the chapter. Select one which you would like to discuss. Select one you would like to hear someone else discuss. Frame a question you want to ask in class.

4. Read the discussion questions and problems at the end of the chapter. Decide on how you would answer them. Frame questions about them.

5. Ask yourself: "If I were preparing a test on this chapter, what would I ask? Which points did the authors seem to emphasize?"

---

*If books are the property of the school instead of the individual students, the students should not be urged to write in them. Instead, have the students record key words and important ideas in a notebook.

PROPER STUDY PROCEDURES

Weak reading skills and ineffective use of the textbook are not the only how-to-study deficiencies many students bring to basic business classes. The teacher should not make the mistake of assuming that "surviving" to reach high school is an index of students' ability to study effectively. The fact is that amazing numbers of students have never received any real help in this most important area.

Because of the nature of the basic business subjects, as has been noted earlier in this chapter, students must utilize a variety of good study techniques. They must know how to use library materials, how to prepare for class participation, how to review systematically, and how to prepare for (and take) written tests or examinations. Therefore, the teacher of basic business subjects can well afford to spend class time during the early part of the school year with special instruction in effective study procedures. Some teachers like to devote one lesson in this manner every week or two during the first grading period.

As an aid in assessing students' present practices, the checklist type of inventory makes a good starting place. It may also be used in follow-up evaluations after the students have had an opportunity to put good practices into operation.

Three inventories which the teacher may use with students are included here: Inventory of Class Participation, Inventory on Reviewing, and Inventory on Taking Examinations.

Inventory of Class Participation

Directions: After each statement, write the word that best
describes your practices: seldom, sometimes,
or usually.

1. Before coming to class, I have done the
homework assignment for the day.   _____

2. When working with a committee, I contribute
to the discussion and planning.   _____

3. When I give an incorrect reply in class, I
try to understand why I am wrong and correct
my mistake.   _____

4. I try not to monopolize the time in class
but to make some contribution each day.   _____

5. I carefully make notes of my assignments at
the time they are given.   _____

6. I do not make distracting noises during the
class period.   _____

7. I prepare specific questions on matters I
do not understand.   _____

8. I try to supplement the textbook using
library resources.   _____

9. I volunteer for special reports that require
out-of-class preparation.   _____

10. I give close attention to class discussion.   _____

11. I ask questions about material that I do not
understand.   _____

12. I listen carefully for special points the
teacher emphasizes and make notes of those
written on the board.   _____

13. I take the responsibility for making up
work I have missed.   _____

14. When the teacher questions my classmates,
I listen and try to answer the questions
in my own mind.   _____

15. I try to think of other examples of or applications for the principles being discussed.

_____

Inventory on Reviewing

<u>Directions</u>: After each statement, write the word that best describes your practices: <u>seldom</u>, <u>sometimes</u>, or <u>usually</u>.

1. I begin review procedures early, allowing time to give unhurried and adequate attention to all parts of the subject. _____

2. I review systematically at least twice each week. _____

3. I review occasionally with one or two of my classmates. _____

4. I "overlearn" material that I want to remember. _____

5. I make a detailed outline of the material to be studied and include in this the minor points relating to the main subject matter. _____

6. I watch for the key ideas, facts, and points emphasized by my instructor and include them in my notes. _____

7. I express in my own words what I have learned. _____

8. I study the main or general ideas in my textbook and then look for subordinate points. _____

9. I keep all corrected test papers and use them in my reviews. _____

10. I test myself on what I actually know concerning the subject matter. _____

11. I find out what type of test is to be given so as to know how to prepare for it. _____

12. I prepare and maintain a test-study schedule. _____

13. If I have trouble understanding something that may be included in a test, I ask the teacher for help. _____

14. I ask myself questions and verify my answers when it is possible to do so. _____

15. I review briefly before each test the material covered since the last test. _____

16. After a test I make sure I know the correct answers to the questions I missed. _____

Inventory on Taking Examinations

Directions: After each statement, write the word that best describes your practices: <u>seldom</u>, <u>sometimes</u>, or <u>usually</u>.

1. I supply myself ahead of time with adequate writing materials. _____

2. I am careful to be on time for a test so that I am relaxed when it begins. _____

3. I make myself physically comfortable and deliberately relax while the exam is being handed out. _____

4. I listen carefully to any instructions given by the teacher. _____

5. I scan the test, giving attention to questions of most importance so that I can budget my time and cover the complete test. _____

6. I read carefully, noting important or key phrases and words before answering questions. _____

7. I outline and organize my thoughts and main points before answering an essay question. _____

8. I try to use correct grammar, punctuation, and spelling, and I try to write legibly. _____

9. I write concisely, underlining key words, numbering points, and outlining main ideas to show relationships. _____

10. On true-false items, I look for the word or phrase which makes the statement true or false. _____

11. On multiple-choice items, I first eliminate the most unlikely possibilities. _____

12. I try to allow time at the end of the period to reread my answers. _____

QUESTIONS, ACTIVITIES, AND PROJECTS

1. What are the chief objectives of a course in business law?

2. Contrast the teaching methods used when teaching basic business subjects with those used when teaching vocational courses.

3. What areas of study skills are of special significance in basic business classes?

4. Explain several ways a teacher might incorporate "study procedures" in a basic business class.

5. How does individual research contribute to student learning?

6. How does an immediate review help students retain what they have learned?

7. How does repetition aid students in retaining what they have learned?

8. Prepare a list of objectives for a course in business economics to be taught to junior and senior students.

9. Prepare an inventory for assessing student use of the library.

10. Teachers cannot rely on all students to review systematically. List a number of ways that teachers can lead students in review activities. These are given as a starter:

    a. Supply students with a list of review questions. (Actually, the list might well be compiled from questions the students have furnished.)

    b. Have students outline selected text material and answer the questions in the text that pertain to the material outlined.

Imitation!
Repetition!
Association!
Participation!

CHAPTER 2

Psychology of Learning in
Basic Business Classes

The psychology of learning is concerned with effecting changes in the behavior of students. These changes are brought about by interactions between persons or between persons and their environment. In business education the attempt is to bring about desirable changes in behavior that will help students adjust wisely to their business environment and to improve upon it. In basic business classes the chief concern is with changes in attitude, appreciation, conduct, understanding, and knowledge.

Many books have been written dealing with the psychology of learning. Obviously, a detailed discussion of learning theories cannot be attempted here. Rather, a brief review of some basic theories and an explanation of what might be called <u>basic principles of learning</u> follow. This list will be restricted to those principles on which there appears to be general agreement among psychologists. It is intended to serve as a refresher or review rather than as a comprehensive treatment of learning.

LEARNING THEORY

One of the earliest learning theories was <u>learning by association</u>. It was stated by Aristotle--something learned earlier is recalled because it is associated with something being experienced now. Pavlov developed this idea into a formula for learning; namely, there exist a number of natural connections between stimuli and responses. Learning has occurred when new stimuli occur <u>along</u> <u>with</u> <u>the</u> <u>original</u> <u>stimulus</u>, then thereafter the new stimuli bring about the expected response (without the presence and aid of the original stimulus). Actually, Pavlov referred to this as "conditioning," since the learning procedure was to establish "conditions" whereby a new stimulus would elicit the response previously attained by the unconditioned stimulus. This stimulus-response theory of learning is often referred to as behavioristic or conditioning psychology.

Behaviorist psychologists believe that learning results in changes in behavior that may be observed. They hold that learning is determined to a large degree by the environment.

Thorndike was a behaviorist psychologist who saw <u>reward</u> <u>as</u> <u>being</u> <u>the</u> <u>most</u> <u>influential</u> <u>principle</u> <u>of</u> <u>learning</u>. B. F. Skinner of Harvard University is a strong proponent of the behavior theory of learning. He states that the components of the behavior theory are <u>stimulus</u>, <u>response</u>, and <u>consequence</u>. According to the behaviorist theory, every element of human thought and feeling may be defined in terms of <u>reinforcement</u>.

According to the Gestalt or cognitive theory, learning is a mental process referred to as information processing. Gestaltists hold that the <u>insight</u> <u>of</u> <u>learners</u> <u>causes</u> <u>them</u> <u>to</u> <u>respond</u> <u>to</u> <u>stimuli</u> <u>as</u> <u>a</u> <u>whole</u>. Learning is influenced by both psychological and physiological conditions. The information processing theory is concerned with how people take in and use information of various kinds. Cognitive psychologists believe that adults learn differently from children because their insight capabilities are more highly developed.

Humanists view learning as a <u>function</u> <u>of</u> <u>the</u> <u>whole</u> <u>person</u>. They believe that when learning occurs, both the intellect and the emotions of the learner are involved. They hold that the incentive for learning comes from within the learner. They also believe that persons, to a large degree, determine their own behavior rather than responding to outside (or environmental) controls.

The humanist, Carl R. Rogers, sets forth these principles of learning:[1]

> Human beings have a natural desire to learn, a natural curiosity about the world, and an eagerness to explore and assimilate new experiences.
>
> Learning is significant--and faster--when the subject is relevant to the learner; witness the adolescent learning to drive a car.
>
> Learning is enhanced by a reduction of external threats.
>
> Participative learning is far more effective than passive learning. Students learn more when learning is self-directed.
>
> Self-initiated learning which involves the whole person of the learner--feelings as well as intellect--is the most lasting and pervasive.
>
> Independence, creativity, and self-reliance are all enhanced by self-evaluation; evaluation by others is of secondary importance. Students must take responsibility for their own learning.

Jerome S. Bruner suggests that, rather than being concerned with theories of learning, teachers should be more concerned with theories of instruction. Theories of learning explain what happens after the fact, while theories of instruction attempt to guide the learners toward the desired goal. In other words, a theory of instruction is concerned with how a thing can best be

---

[1]Carl R. Rogers, _Freedom to Learn_. Columbus, Ohio: Merrill, 1969, pp. 129 and 130.

learned. Bruner gives the following as the major features of a
theory of instruction:[2]

1. It should specify the experiences which
    most effectively implant in the individ-
    ual a pre-disposition toward learning.

2. It should specify the ways in which a
    body of knowledge should be structured so
    that it can be most readily grasped by
    the learner.

3. It should specify the most effective se-
    quences in which to present the materials
    to be learned.

4. It should specify the nature and pacing
    of rewards and punishments in the process
    of learning and teaching.

Some principles of learning and instruction that bring about
effective classroom teaching are given on the following pages.
These principles should be of practical help to basic business
teachers.

SOME PRINCIPLES OF LEARNING

1. <u>Students learn from observation and imitation</u>. Imitation is probably the most primitive form of learning. It is certainly one of the earliest forms of learning utilized by young
children. Many persons try to imitate those whom they respect.
Young children imitate their parents and students imitate their
teachers. It is not expected that the students' enthusiasm,
standards of neatness, and patterns of organization and work will
excel those set by their teachers. However, it is important for
teachers to set high standards for their students through their

---

[2]Jerome S. Bruner, <u>Toward a Theory of Instruction</u>. Cambridge,
Mass.: The Belknap Press of Harvard University Press, 1966, p. 40.

24

own behavior. For example, the teachers' work at the chalkboard and with transparencies should be the very best.

2. <u>Students</u> <u>hit</u> <u>more</u> <u>targets</u> <u>when</u> <u>they</u> <u>aim</u> <u>at</u> <u>them</u>. Human behavior is essentially purposeful or goal seeking. So learning has its maximum value when it is planned to achieve specific goals.

It is not sufficient for teachers to know the objectives of any lesson. The students also must understand them, accept them, and consider them worthy. If student learning is to be effective, teachers must be careful to see that there are achievable goals.

In order to hold student interest and prevent discouragement, teachers must make sure that there are short-term goals as well as long-term goals. It is sometimes helpful to set intermediate dates by which certain objectives are to be reached as well as a final due date. Success in this matter of establishing goals is no doubt one of the most important roles of the persons who guide student learning activities.

3. <u>Students</u> <u>learn</u> <u>from</u> <u>experience</u>. Active participation is far better than passive reception. Or, as John Dewey worded this principle: "We learn to do by doing." Probably more is learned from firsthand experience than from any other way. Teachers must remember that talking is not necessarily teaching. Their responsibility as teachers is to set up worthwhile, interesting, and challenging learning situations, to assist students as they select experiences, and to guide their learning activities.

4. <u>Learning</u> <u>is</u> <u>most</u> <u>satisfactory</u> <u>when</u> <u>success</u> <u>is</u> <u>assured</u>. Learning experiences should constitute a challenge but not so much of one that objectives cannot be achieved. The ordinary dart board illustrates this principle. If a person hits the bull's-eye every time, there is no challenge. On the other hand, if he is so far from the target that he can never hit it, he soon loses incentive to keep on trying. Teachers must see that tasks and materials are at the proper maturity levels for students. Teachers cannot expect all students to perform identical activities, nor accomplish the

25

same purposes with equal degrees of success. The task then is to provide a sufficient variety of activities which are at different difficulty levels.

5. Learning is enhanced when reinforcement is direct and immediate. Rewards are much more effective than punishment. Punishment does not help a student find the correct answer, and it may lead to discouragement. Rewards reinforce responses and are most effective when they occur immediately. In this way there is no doubt in a student's mind as to the relationship between the reward and his response. One of the chief values of "programmed materials" is the reinforcement that comes immediately from knowing that one's answer is correct. A learner becomes anxious to proceed to the next step in his learning experience. Praise of work well done is one of the most valuable forms of rewards in learning and one of the easiest to use.

Teachers should grade and return students' papers as soon as possible after the work is turned in. Much of the effectiveness of going over examination papers is lost if there is considerable delay in returning them to the students.

6. Learning is effective when the material being studied is meaningful. Information is most meaningful when it is useful and is most useful when it can be applied immediately after it has been learned. The basic business subjects are loaded with informamation people need in their everyday living. It has already been pointed out that learning is most meaningful when students understand the material they are studying. The business experiences students have already had enable them to appreciate the value of what they are studying.

7. Transfer of learning to new situations is increased if teachers teach for transfer. The transfer of learning is at the hub of the teaching process. Specifics are not as important as broad concepts which can be applied to new problem situations. Teachers must be concerned with those fundamental understandings that give structure to the subject being studied. Teaching in-

dividual topics without placing them in the context of the broader field of knowledge of which a particular course is a part defeats the purpose of the transfer of learning.

The application of principles must be taught in addition to the presentation of facts. Both facts and principles should be taught in relation to as many important daily life situations as possible. Students should be taught to search for and find identical or similar factors in two or more situations or cases. The transfer to new problems will be greatest when teachers have guided students in discovering relationships for themselves and applying principles to many different situations.

8. <u>Learning</u> <u>is</u> <u>retained</u> <u>better</u> <u>and</u> <u>longer</u> <u>if</u> <u>it</u> <u>is</u> <u>repeated</u> <u>or</u> <u>reviewed</u>. Material is quickly forgotten when it is first learned. In fact, much of it is lost within a short time unless conscious efforts are made to retain it. Reviews that come shortly after material is learned slow down the forgetting process. Fortunately, information can be relearned in much less time than was required to learn it the first time. If it is relearned or reviewed frequently at increasingly longer intervals, it may be remembered almost indefinitely. Most students do not review material systematically or automatically, so teachers must provide periodic reviews for them.

9. <u>Learning</u> <u>is</u> <u>not</u> <u>restricted</u> <u>to</u> <u>planned</u> <u>objectives</u>. Experiences planned to accomplish a particular objective may achieve unintended outcomes which may be positive or negative. For example, if a student's contributions are continually ignored, he soon learns that they are neither appreciated nor welcomed. Teachers must encourage all class members to contribute to class activities; they must also accept the efforts of all students and lead their students to do the same.

10. <u>Learning</u> <u>is</u> <u>enhanced</u> <u>when</u> <u>there</u> <u>is</u> <u>stimulation</u> <u>without</u> <u>coercion</u>. Authoritarian leadership causes group members to depend too heavily on the leader. Excessive direction by the teacher leads to conformity and stifles initiative, self-confidence, and

creativity. Freedom in participation on the part of students stimulates curiosity and a desire for further learning.

11. <u>Learning</u> <u>is</u> <u>effective</u> <u>when</u> <u>material</u> <u>is</u> <u>presented</u> <u>visually</u>. Student interest and motivation can be sustained through the wise use of audio-visual methods and materials. The teacher must always remember that the visual is an "aid" in the teaching process and is not the whole process. A slide presentation, for example, might be used as the means to introduce a new topic, to raise questions about a subject, to clarify a concept, to illustrate through examples, or to review previously covered material.

It must be supplemented with comments from the teacher and discussion by the class members. Almost any class presentation can be improved by including in one's lesson plan some type of audio-visual materials.

ASSURING POSITIVE STUDENT BEHAVIOR

The best way to provide for positive student behavior is to plan a full period of meaningful activity. This is the payoff for teachers being thorough in their lesson planning. Students apply themselves to learning when they are active and their achievement is meaningful.

On the other hand, students who lack the challenge of tasks which are acceptable to them seek other outlets for their interests.

Coping with discipline problems is one of the most trying aspects of teaching and one of great concern to potential teachers. Discipline problems are usually responses which occur from lack of proper incentive or from improper stimuli in the classroom en-vironment. A teacher who is careful to provide an environment in which students feel comfortable and challenged will diminish greatly opportunities for problems to develop.

Experienced teachers have offered several suggestions which new teachers can use to prevent discipline problems.

Establishing Legitimate Assignments

The objectives established for the class should be related to the students in a manner that they will understand. They should know what is expected of them. All classroom assignments should be directly related to the stated objectives. They should be reasonable in length and within each student's ability. Timing is also important--requiring a lengthy assignment to be completed on the same evening as a major school function (such as a basketball game) is expecting more than will be forthcoming.

Explaining Grading Policies

Grading policies should be made clear when the assignment is made--not after it has been completed and submitted to the teacher. Grading should be consistent with the policies established. For example, if the grading policy for written reports states that five or more spelling errors will decrease the report grade by 10 points, the teacher who disregards this policy on the first report assigned but adheres to it on the second report is setting the stage for a discipline problem.

Exerting Proper Authority

The teacher _is_ the authority in the classroom. This should be established at the beginning of the school term. A set of classroom rules should be discussed during the first week of class and followed throughout the term. These rules may include school rules, classroom do's and don'ts, and due dates for homework. Penalties for failure to follow the rules may also be established.

A teacher can be a friend to the students without being their "buddy." A teacher may feel that using slang, dressing like the students, or allowing students to address him on a first-name basis is a means of gaining rapport with students. This teacher will find, however, that the students then resent any attempt that their "buddy" makes to express authority or to curb behavior problems.

True authority exists where respect for authority is recognized. Teachers who exhibit a respect for rules and authority themselves are more apt to gain the respect of their students. It is very easy for a student to say, "Why should I pay any attention to your rules? You don't pay any attention to the school's rules!"

Encouraging Student Activity

Hands and minds which are busy at constructive tasks are not likely to induce problems. Students should be involved in a meaningful activity at the moment the class period begins. The teacher must not allow time for students to become engaged in lengthy personal conversations because class discussion will be regarded as an interruption. The teacher should assign the task the day before, write it on the board or on a handout before class, play a recording, or present information in some other way--immediately.

A student who is bored may look for some problematic means of reducing that boredom. The teacher should vary the classroom activities and keep the students motivated as well as busy. Asking the students to answer the questions at the end of the chapter repeatedly is not very motivating. Students may find it more interesting to entertain themselves or their classmates in some other manner, thus creating a problem.

Knowing the Subject Matter

Students have little respect for the teacher who is continually making mistakes and who is unable to answer their questions. Consequently, "stumping-and-bluffing the teacher" may become a classroom game.

If students are not challenged by the classroom activity, a discipline problem may develop. Likewise, if students perceive the instruction as too complex for their understanding, a problem may be forthcoming. Understanding and dealing with individual differences are discussed to a greater extent in Chapter 4.

The good teacher is enthusiastic about the subject matter being taught. This enthusiasm should come easily to the teacher of basic business subjects because of the relevancy of the subject matter to the students' everyday lives. Enthusiasm is contagious, and once students become enthusiastic about the class discussion, assignment, or activity, they are less likely to become involved in negative or non-contributing activities.

Endeavoring to Be a "Nice" Person

"We really like our science teacher, Mrs. Smith. She's so nice!" This is a familiar comment made by high school students. While the students may not know anything about Mrs. Smith's personal life, they recognize her as a nice person because of her classroom activities.

Mrs. Smith is objective and fair in dealing with controversial situations. She allows the students to discuss the advantages and disadvantages of situations under study. (Examples in basic business would be labor unions and government regulations on businesses.) She listens to students' ideas and respects their right to their opinions, even though they disagree with hers.

The students would probably say that Mrs. Smith is not prejudiced in her attitudes. Most individuals acquire prejudices of some type during their lifetimes. It is important that, as adults, individuals overcome those prejudices. Teachers should be careful not to let their prejudices show. Students should be treated equally despite any differences in their physical, social, or intellectual characteristics.

It is probably safe to say that Mrs. Smith doesn't "put down" the younger generation. She condemns neither their dress nor their music, and she does not imply that the world will be in jeopardy when her students enter the working world.

Most importantly, Mrs. Smith has probably developed the ability to laugh at herself and admit her mistakes. Students find it uninteresting to laugh "at" a teacher who laughs at himself.

When a teacher is able to say, "I never have any behavior problems in my classroom," it is likely that a conscious effort has been made to prevent such problems through wise planning and developing good interpersonal relationships.

CLASS GROUPING FOR STUDENT INTERACTION

Learning does not take place in a vacuum but in relationship to other individuals and one's environment. It is the interaction among members of small face-to-face groups that provides the setting in which significant changes in attitudes and habits take place. Learning involves far more than the mastery of facts. A desirable interactive learning situation respects feelings and attitudes which may be more significant than the words which are spoken.

The teacher is the key person in establishing a situation in which communication can take place effectively and which promotes free interaction within a group of learners and between groups. The situation must be free from personal threats, and every effort must be made to hear, understand, and respect the responses of every member of the group.

Forces of Attraction

The wise teacher will continually evaluate the attractiveness of his class as a group. Some of the forces of attraction by which the teacher can make such evaluations are group goals, group activity, democratic group organization, individual recognition, and student security.

Group Goals. The group is attractive when the goals of the group are compatible with those of the individual and when there is harmony of purpose within the group--when a person feels that he "belongs."

Group Activities. The group is attractive when individual members agree with the program of work to be done and feel pleased to participate in it. Interest in the group's activities is often associated with liking the people in it. When persons are actively involved in the work of a group, they have good reason to support it.

Group Organization and Leadership. The democratic process which provides for friendly participation usually makes a group attractive. Most students react negatively to authoritarianism. At the opposite extreme, a group in which each person goes his own way soon loses its attractiveness. So the democratic organizational pattern, with discreet teacher guidance and true student sharing, appears to be the preferred pattern.

Good leadership in group processes encourages wide participation--it is a substitute for autocratic procedures. Leadership is brought about through democratic procedures. When positions of responsibility are awarded to individuals through group action, it helps students develop initiative and wholesome attitudes.

Desire for Recognition. Almost every person evaluates himself by the standards of his group. He "sees himself" in some definite relationship with his fellows. For a group to be attractive the individual must know where he stands and be satisfied with that standing.

<u>Need</u> <u>for</u> <u>Security</u>. Security is found in trust. <u>Therefore</u>, <u>the</u> <u>group</u> <u>which</u> <u>can</u> <u>be</u> <u>trusted</u> <u>is</u> <u>attractive</u>. A person is insecure with a group only if he cannot trust it, and he will become involved in the life of the group only to the extent to which he feels "safe." It is absurd for a teacher to expect a student to express himself freely if he feels he will be misunderstood or that his expressions will not be accepted.

Teachers who are concerned about the security of their students begin with "the known" and proceed with a series of activities that constitute challenges, yet make for successful achievement.

The group process should, in time, change the behavior of learners. When a person becomes concerned about the problems of his group, he learns--both as an individual and as a group member. He appreciates other group members and respects their points of view as they all share in making group decisions.

The attractiveness of any group for its members depends on the needs of each individual member and the way the group goes about meeting those needs. A student will choose to stay with a group as long as the forces of attraction are greater than those of disruption. As the teacher evaluates his class by these standards, he can easily see how each one contributes to his effectiveness as a teacher. By these standards, the most attractive class is the one where learning is the most effective.

THE ROLES OF THE TEACHER IN LEARNING

Having reviewed some of the fundamental principles of learning, it seems appropriate at this point to enumerate the functions that together constitute the principal teaching-learning roles of the basic business teacher. The teacher:

1. Orients students to the course and to each new unit topic.

2. Is responsible for creating conditions in which a climate or atmosphere exists that encourages the development of fruitful interaction--a climate that provides freedom to explore, to question, to differ, to create.

3. Sees that there are worthy goals and purposes for the course and each unit topic.

4. Motivates students to want to learn--interests and inspires students to participate in active learning experiences.

5. Provides for differentiation in student goals and learning experiences adaptable to varying levels of maturity, readiness, interest, and ability.

6. Helps in the selection and creation of learning activities--active participation in preference to passive.

7. Stimulates and coordinates the work of individuals and groups without domination or coercion, utilizing democratic controls.

8. Serves as a resource person--furnishes materials, references, and sources.

9. Guides in the use of community resources.

10. Provides for variety in methods, techniques, procedures, and learning activities.

11. Sees that student achievement is observable, immediate, and rewarded.

12. Evaluates student progress and guides students in self-evaluation.

The discussion in succeeding chapters gives numerous examples, illustrations, and devices to aid the basic business teacher in carrying out these roles effectively.

QUESTIONS, ACTIVITIES, AND PROJECTS

1. "Experience and materials must be at the maturity level of the students." What significance does this have for the teacher?

2. What factors make a group attractive? Explain the importance that these factors have on the members of the group.

3. Select one of the accepted principles of learning and give an example of how you would apply it in a basic business class.

4. How may a teacher bring a withdrawn student into class participation?

5. React to this statement--"A person wants above all else to have a personal feeling of worthwhileness and self-respect. This want is so strong that it serves as the motivation for more action than all other wants together (excepting the want of survival)."

6. One of the fundamental principles of learning is that rewards are much more effective than punishment. Explain how a teacher can reward students, including those whose work is not of the highest caliber.

7. The following are some of the needs of adolescents. Select five of those listed, and for each one chosen write its implications for basic business teachers.

   a. To accept and adjust to the physical changes taking place in their bodies.

   b. To adjust to living and working with those of the opposite sex.

   c. To develop a code of ethics and a philosophy of life.

   d. To develop individuality and less dependence on the peer group.

   e. To strengthen the ability to generate new ideas and to rationalize.

   f. To explore vocational opportunities of promise.

   g. To become an active part of an environment controlled largely by adults.

   h. To become an active participant in society, both economically and socially.

   i. To face up to the need for further education.

8. Suggest several ways that teachers may learn more about the characteristics and behavior of adolescents. Here are two starters:

   a. By generally observing groups of young people.

   b. By making a case study of a particular adolescent.

9. Select five of the learning principles reviewed in this chapter and indicate specific implications each one has for teachers of basic business classes.

10. Explain several ways that a teacher may develop "learning readiness" on the part of his students.

11. Select one of the teacher "roles" enumerated in this chapter and write a paragraph explaining how you would perform this role as a basic business teacher.

Students are apathetic towards learning when it is obvious that the teacher is uninterested in teaching.

CHAPTER 3

Motivating Student Interest

When do persons most actively seek to learn something? When they really want to know the answer! A person will call someone else, look in the encyclopedia, or make a trip to the library when he really "wants to know"! It's this "want-to-ness" on the part of students that will be covered in this chapter. How do successful teachers stimulate this interest on the part of their students?

Motivation is the real force behind learning. It is the mainspring of effort, the incentive for human behavior. Motivation is indeed the key to effective teaching and learning.

The principles of motivation include the following:
Students:

1. Need to succeed.
2. Need to develop a self-concept.
3. Desire to be competent.
4. Wish to control their environment.
5. Can be motivated by interesting subject matter which provokes thought.

Students are motivated the most when there is a happy balance between:

1. The unknown and the familiar.
2. Challenge and the promise of success.

Motives may be general or specific, natural or artificial. Learning that is encouraged by natural interest is preferable to learning under extrinsic motivation. So in the discussion here the emphasis will be given to stimulating learning through natural or intrinsic motivation.

Many things contribute to intrinsic motivation. Five basic factors will be considered here: stimulation of curiosity, use of variety, satisfaction from accomplishment, motivation through visuals, and stimulation through praise.

AROUSING STUDENT CURIOSITY

Human beings are naturally curious. Begin telling a story and in the middle of it hesitate, then say, "But you wouldn't be interested!" If it is a good story, everyone will immediately beg you to continue. Everyone is anxious to hear the end result. This is what the teacher wants to do in the classroom: create a desire on the part of students to want to know more.

Using Case Stories

One of the best ways to make students want to learn is through "story telling." Everyone likes a story, especially if it actually happened. It is most effective when "it happened right here in our own community," when it is most unusual, or when it illustrates vividly either the right way or the wrong way to do something.

For example, consider the story of the vagrant who was taken into custody for loitering. After his arrest he reported that he made it a practice to sleep in vacant buildings in the business area. In spite of the extremely cold weather (a low temperature for the night of 8 degrees) he had only his overcoat and a blanket of newspapers to keep him warm. The police felt that they had done him a favor in locking him up in the warm city jail. Then, upon searching his clothing, the police officers discovered a bank book that indicated he had $7,947 in a local bank, deposited

over a ten-year period. The smallest deposit recorded was $420.
(This is a true story reported on the front page of the Cincinnati
Post, under the caption: "Vagrant's Pockets Lined with 'Green.'")

Such an unusual story naturally arouses interest and whets
the appetite. It not only serves the purpose of introducing the
topic of savings in an interesting way but also vividly illustrates
both good and poor savings methods. It is good to invest one's
savings at interest but unwise to carry large sums of cash on
one's person.

An excellent way to lead students to "look for answers" is
by using the case story to develop a problem situation that calls
for further research. For example, there is the case of Richard
Cone whose monthly bank statement showed his balance to be $60
less than it should have been. Among his canceled checks was one
made payable to James Allen, which Richard had not written.

James Allen had lived in the same house with Richard Cone and
had often visited him in his room. He had learned the name of
Richard's bank and had secured a copy of Dick's signature. Before
leaving the city he had forged Richard's name on a check, made it
payable to himself, and cashed it in a local clothing store.

At this point the teacher may stop the "story" and ask:
"Who will stand this loss?" Usually there will be at least three
different opinions: Richard Cone, the bank, and the clothing
store. Someone might suggest that James Allen would be caught
and have to make it good.

Instead of giving the correct answer at this point, the
teacher asks for volunteers to learn the correct answer and report back to the class the following day. Among those who have
already offered opinions, someone will volunteer, for that student
wants to be able to tell the class tomorrow that the information
was correct. Any student whose brother, sister, father, or mother
is an attorney or banker is likely to volunteer, also.

The story motivates interest and is used to lead to research
or personal interviews--good learning experiences in either case.

Using Local Happenings

Here is an example of using a local happening to arouse curiosity when introducing the study of automobile insurance.

The teacher, Miss Jones, is standing in the front of her classroom. Classes are changing, and there is a great hubbub among the students as they enter the room. As the bell rings, the news spills right into the lesson period.

"Miss Jones, Robert Meece will not be back to school for several weeks," says James, taking his seat in the second row near the windows.

"That's right," adds Helen. "You see he is in Central Hospital. I understand he was hurt seriously in an accident and his car was ruined."

"It wasn't his fault, either," remarks Harold. "Will the driver of the other car have to pay the doctor and the hospital bills?"

Robert Meece had been injured in an automobile accident the evening before. One of his legs was in a cast, and he had several bad cuts and bruises on his shoulder and arms. He would be in the hospital for several days; then there would be weeks of recuperation at home. He would have to learn to walk on crutches before he could return to school.

An unhappy affair! Yes, but what a wonderful time to launch the class on its study of automobile insurance!

James, Helen, and Harold have interested everyone in this subject of automobile insurance. All are interested in Robert's recovery, to be sure; but they want to know more, to learn the answers to their questions. Harold's question was a good one, "Will the driver of the other car have to pay the doctor and the hospital bills?" The students really wanted to know. The brief discussion which followed led to other questions, too, whose answers they wished to learn:

1. Does Robert have a driver's license?
2. Were there any witnesses to the accident?
3. Was the accident reported to the police right away?
4. Who was responsible? Does it make a difference?
5. Was Robert's car insured? Was the other car insured?
6. Were others injured?
7. Will Robert's parent or guardian have to sue the owner of the other car to get payment for the damages, or does the insurance company do the suing? Does anybody have to sue?

Using the Newspaper

The newspaper is an excellent source of stories, general information, and specific data of great value for stimulating interest in basic business subjects. An account of a court action growing out of an accident on the golf course will help introduce the topic of public liability insurance. An ad offering for sale an automobile that has been repossessed for failure to keep up the payments can be used to arouse curiosity about instalment purchases. A report of a large sum of money being stolen from a person's wallet, or from his home, makes an excellent illustration to create interest in the topics of using money substitutes or keeping cash and other valuables safe. An ad about the local Family Budget Service is timely for motivating interest in money management.

Many newspapers provide special services to schools, such as discount rates, supplementary learning materials, and special sections and editions, free of charge. A teacher of basic business subjects should check with the local newspaper office to learn what services may be available for classroom use.

Introducing New Topics When They Are Timely

Almost any topic in any basic business textbook can be introduced in a dozen different ways and at many different times during the school year. True, some topics are interrelated, with one of them leading right into the other, and skipping about in the book may break that close articulation. But the added zest in studying that comes from true interest by the students more than compensates for the loss (real or imagined) that comes from breaking the lock step arrangement of textbook materials.

Teachers will not want to be desultory in skipping around in the textbook. Rather, seeing what units are forthcoming, they will plan ahead, being alert for events that may be used as lead-ins for the units not yet introduced. But teachers should not hesitate to switch the sequence when something especially pertinent occurs, such as when the family of one of the students moves to Alaska, another's house burns, or someone is involved in an automobile accident such as that previously described.

MOTIVATING THROUGH VARIETY

Teachers who respond positively to the challenge of the basic business courses vary their daily programs. Someone has said that "variety is the spice of life," and this is doubly true in basic business classes. Regardless of what one's favorite form of entertainment is, he doesn't want to experience that all the time. Everyone likes a change, and this is particularly true in the classroom.

Some of the different types of student activities that may be utilized are interviews, field trips, oral and written reports, notebooks, community resource persons, panels, debates, check-lists, pretests, case problems, dramatizations, buzz sessions, committee projects, and current events. Most of these activities

will be discussed more fully in succeeding lessons. By using a
checklist of all types of desirable activities, one can be sure
that he will have variety in his program.

The Committee Field Trip

Any teacher or student who has experienced a well-planned
field trip will attest to its value. In addition to being planned,
its purpose must, of course, be closely related to the unit topic
currently being studied by the class.

The chief roadblocks to class field trips are transportation
difficulties and the limited time available. It may be difficult
or impossible to schedule a school bus or arrange for an adequate
number of cars. Also, a single class period hardly affords sufficient time for travel to and from the business, in addition to
observation at the business.

The best solution toward overcoming these difficulties seems
to be the committee field trip. Two or three students make the
excursion and report to the class on what they saw. Colored
slides of key observation points may serve to heighten the interest and value of the committee report. In some instances role
playing may also be utilized. During the year every student
should be given the opportunity to experience one or more group
trips. It will contribute much toward achieving variety in any
basic business class.

Preparing the Resource Person

The occasional use of a resource person is another excellent
way to add variety in the classroom. Perhaps the error most frequently committed in utilizing a resource speaker is neglecting
to prepare him for his visit. He should know something about the
type of class being visited and the students who constitute the

class. A visiting speaker should know what part of the content of a unit topic has already been studied by the class--whether he is launching the topic or appearing during or at the conclusion of the study of the unit. It is especially helpful if he can be given some specific subtopics to discuss and/or some questions to be answered. He should be told exactly where he should report when he arrives at the school and who will greet him there.

The teacher may give the resource person the following set of guidelines, which has proved helpful to speakers in local high schools:

Guidelines for Resource Persons

1. Be yourself. Use methods, techniques, and media with which you are familiar.

2. Tell something about your background as a businessman, and include some concrete examples showing how the discussion topic applies to your business.

3. Present your own experiences, discuss your business problems, and express personal opinions. Students want to know what you think and how you react in the everyday business world.

4. Portray your ideas visually when possible.

5. Use vocabulary, terminology, and definitions on the level of the students without "talking down" to them.

6. Keep the students involved. Accept the students as equals. Adopt an attitude of open communication with the students. Give them an opportunity to ask questions and express their opinions.

7. Develop a thought pattern or a general outline of the subject to be covered. Think of the things students might want to know.

8. Name some periodicals or trade magazines you rely on for information as a businessman. If possible, let the students examine sample periodicals you find useful.

9. Limit your presentation to not more than 35 or 40 minutes.

10. Refrain from using profanity.

SUCCESS MOTIVATES STUDENTS

The adage, "Nothing succeeds like success," is of enormous significance in motivating students in basic business subjects. Continuous success builds confidence and spurs students to further achievement. This is accomplished by meeting individual differences, seeing that students know what they are aiming toward, and guiding students in undertaking problems that are within their capabilities.

Meeting Individual Differences

Meeting individual differences is developed in detail in Chapter 4. The importance of varying assignments at different levels of difficulty is discussed, and specific suggestions for helping teachers motivate and challenge both slow learners and superior students are presented. Meeting individual differences is essential to strong motivation for learning.

Knowledge and Attainment of Goals

Nearly all human behavior is essentially purposeful or goal seeking. If students are to be motivated to undertake meaningful activities, they must know what their objectives are--what is expected of them. As mentioned in Chapter 2, the goals most readily accepted by students are those they set for themselves.

Equally important to an understanding and acceptance of goals is the satisfaction that comes from reaching them. Regardless of how worthy an objective may be, a student becomes discouraged unless he can see his progress toward reaching it. The average person who starts to climb a high mountain will soon quit if he feels that it is impossible to reach the summit. Any long project will hold its participant only as long as he can observe that he is achieving.

So the teacher needs to make sure that there are short-term goals as well as long-term objectives. If a teacher lived two miles from the school where he teaches and was to walk home, how would he proceed? Would he head for "home" or wouldn't he first set out for that turn a few blocks down the road? Then upon reaching it, he would head next for that large brick building a half mile away, etc. For a major project several stepping stones should be established along the way. In some cases tentative dates might be set for achieving specific milestones. In this way interest is maintained, and one's observable accomplishments motivate him to keep moving ahead.

Tasks Should Be Challenging but Achievable

All learning activities should <u>not</u> be short and easy. Very little learning is gained through tasks that are not challenging enough to demand one's best. Ideally, assignments should be achievable and at the same time challenging. When playing darts, a participant's greatest satisfaction comes at the level of maximum challenge. If he is too close to the target, he can't miss and he loses interest; if he is too far away, he can't score and becomes discouraged. <u>The real challenge is at the difficulty level where he can achieve but must exercise his best skill in order to make a creditable showing</u>. And so it is with maintaining interest in basic business subjects.

PICTURES STIMULATE INTEREST

Pictures--both still and motion--are among the best interest stimulators. Watch a young person at a movie who has dropped his glove or cap on the floor. He will reach down and pick it up without taking his eyes off the screen.

Outstanding teachers of basic business classes accumulate a library of bright colorful pictures. Their libraries contain hundreds of pictures so that when one is needed to illustrate a particular subject, it is readily available.

Filmstrips and motion pictures are also available in quantity--many of them free, others at a small rental fee. Teachers' manuals usually supply the names and addresses of sources of films and filmstrips and, in some instances, recommend specific titles.

Slides can be developed by both teachers and students. All that is needed is a camera, colored film, and an alertness to situations that make good classroom illustrations.

With a little expenditure of time and effort teachers can make school work interesting by making it visual. The effective use of visuals is developed more fully in Chapter 5.

RECOGNITION AND PRAISE

The toddler at the swimming pool kept calling, "Watch me, Mother, watch me!" Then after jumping in again he asked, "There, did I do it better?"

What this young fellow wanted was attention and recognition. Of course, he got it--his mother encouraged him by telling him that indeed he did do it better. Thus he kept on trying to do it even better to merit more praise.

Commending a student for work well done is a powerful interest incentive; it creates a climate that enhances one's putting forth his best efforts. It is a strong motivation factor, but it may be used only after one has achieved something for which he can be praised. Teachers can usually find something about a student's work for which he may be commended: its high quality, completeness, thoroughness, neatness, timeliness, originality, appearance, etc. Where the work itself is not praiseworthy, perhaps his attitude is one of willingness, cooperation, or persistence.

It is not to be implied that praise should be given when it is not deserved. Sweeping commendation of all work done, regardless of its quality, soon becomes meaningless and sparks no incentive. Praise for good work does not mean that there is to be no criticism. Criticism is an effective way to improve performance, but to be most effective, it must be specific and constructive. It should be given in a quiet spirit and should always be focused on the work and not on the person.

ENTHUSIASM

Few students can be motivated to a degree that exceeds the interest and enthusiasm of the teacher. When it is obvious that a teacher is bored with his task, student interest evaporates almost instantly. On the other hand, teacher enthusiasm begets student enthusiasm. The teacher who is honestly enthused with his class, and with his subject matter, sparks his students to become involved in meaningful learning activities.

MOVING FROM INTEREST TO ACTIVITY

The purpose of motivation is to lead into student activity. In the early part of this chapter it was pointed out how the story was used as the basis of further learning through follow-up student activity. This was also illustrated in the case of the automobile accident--questions were asked that necessitated student reading and research in order to find answers.

The local paper carries advertisements of banks and building-and-loan associations where interest may be earned on one's savings. But not all institutions pay the same rates of interest on savings. The ads in the local paper may be used to stimulate interest and raise questions.

"Which association pays the highest rate of return?"

"What are the restrictions regarding the making of deposits and withdrawals?"

"Why does one institution pay more than others?"

"Do savings begin to earn interest the day they are deposited and is interest paid to the day of withdrawal? Or must the money remain on deposit a specified period of time in order to earn interest?"

"How often is the interest compounded?"

These and other questions lead to student activity--meaningful activity. A committee may visit the various banks and other institutions and learn answers to such questions. Then, through role playing, the committee members can give a most interesting report of their findings to the remaining members of the class.

Yes, motivation that leads to student activity is the most desirable type.

QUESTIONS, ACTIVITIES, AND PROJECTS

1. What kinds of items would you suggest a basic business teacher include in a file titled Motivation?

2. The role of government in our economy is a topic that students hear discussed all the time. How could you motivate student interest in this topic?

3. What are some specific ways that basic business teachers can provide for individual differences?

4. "Purposeful learning is the key to student interest." How can basic business teachers achieve purposeful learning?

5. How would you praise a student's work and, at the same time, criticize his weak points?

6. Motivating students is probably the teacher's primary function. List several ways that teachers can motivate student interest.

7. "Variety is the spice of life." Explain what basic business teachers can do to make sure that there will be variety in their classes.

8. Select a unit normally taught in economics or business law and describe three approaches you might use to develop student interest in that topic.

9. Describe a local happening that occurred recently in your community that might be used to introduce some unit topic in basic business class.

10. Assume that you plan to invite a credit manager from one of the stores in your community to speak to your students in connection with their study of credit. Would you want him at the beginning or toward the end of their unit study? Why? Explain specifically what you would do to prepare him and your class members for his visit.

11. Students, as consumers, play an important role in business. Explain how the newspaper could be used to arouse interest in their problems as consumers.

12. Prepare a resource directory listing the names and addresses of organizations and persons in your community that might be able to provide you with basic business information, guest speakers, field trips, etc.

*The primary objective of every teacher
is that every student learn.*

CHAPTER 4

Providing for
Student Differences

No two persons are exactly alike, not even identical twins. Even though two individuals may have comparable IQ's and may seem to have similar attitudes, they are really different. Each student is unique in physical characteristics, family background, basic skills, mental aptitude, emotional balance, experiences, and interests.

Because of differences in individuals, students learn at different rates and in different ways. They may even react differently in identical situations. Learning activities that have a strong appeal to some may be looked upon with indifference by others. Some students can read the textbook with considerable insight; others, with little understanding. Some students are eager to participate in class discussions; others are reluctant to take an active part. Some can work with abstract ideas; others can succeed only when working with concrete objects. If all students in a class are to be challenged to the maximum of their potentialities, teachers must be alert to individual differences and make provision for them. Basic business courses offer a wide variety of opportunities for stimulating and challenging learning experiences.

THE PROBLEM OF PROVIDING FOR INDIVIDUAL DIFFERENCES

One of the major concerns of basic business teachers is challenging the good students in a class without losing the interest of those with less ability. To accomplish this, teachers must provide different types of activities for different students. For example, while one student may be doing library research for an oral report and another may be working on a project book, still others (acting as a committee) may be visiting a local business to set up a field trip for the class.

Teachers should keep in mind the fact that academic superiority, as indicated by aptitude in such areas as language usage and abstract reasoning, does not necessarily indicate overall superiority. Although there may be a few students who are good at everything, they are the exceptions.

Every person has special interests and special abilities that distinguish him from others. A poor student in business law or in economics may have artistic talent and can be given assignments that utilize this ability in an acceptable manner, such as preparing posters, bulletin-board exhibits, flow charts, cartoons, etc. A poor student academically may be superior in penmanship or lettering, good at typing, or gifted at making things. A student who has expressed little interest in general business but who has a flair for the theatrical may have his interest sparked by giving him responsibility in a dramatization and role-playing situation. It is the teacher's responsibility to learn about each student's special aptitudes and make use of them. Using a student's special abilities stimulates his interest in the subject matter being studied. It also enables the student to develop his talents further. In most instances, success in one endeavor builds the confidence that helps one succeed in the other tasks undertaken.

The solution to the problem of providing for differences in student abilities lies only partly in having a variety of activities. Perhaps even more significant is the way in which responsibilities are assigned or assumed. For example, in carrying out a community survey the best students in a class can assume leadership roles in planning the project and interpreting the findings. Slower students may be able to collect the data and tabulate it. In carrying out committee projects the best students can guide the planning, lead group discussions, and coordinate the committee's activities. The less able learners can participate in everything the committee does and profit from the guidance of those in leadership roles. They may even assume the responsibility for record keeping and routine activities of the committee.

One effective way to provide for varying interests and abilities of students is through the use of supplementary materials. For example, a browsing table of reading materials should be provided. This material would include not only booklets, pamphlets, and circulars written on a grade level below that of the average of the class, but also books, periodicals, and reports that challenge the best and most advanced readers. In addition, filmstrips should be made available for individual use.

WHO IS SUPERIOR AND WHO IS SLOW?

Every teacher soon recognizes that in almost any class the range in mental ability is considerable. There are some students who stand out above the group as a whole, while others lag behind, unable to keep pace with the majority of the class. Neither do they understand much of the subject matter discussed in the textbook nor do they understand the ideas presented during class discussions.

The Determining Factors

Mental Ability. Research has consistently demonstrated that mental age is the best single index of capacity for success in school work. The IQ range from 90 to 110 is generally considered "average." Approximately 50 to 60 percent of the students enrolled in high school will fall in this "average" range. Approximately 20 percent will fall below it, and a similar percentage will fall above it.

Vocabulary. It is to be expected that students' knowledge of words will vary widely since vocabulary strength is very closely related to intelligence. The average high school student knows approximately 10,000 to 15,000 words, but some students will know 30,000 to 40,000 words. The routine conversation of most people rarely goes beyond 3,000 of the most familiar words, and the vocabularies of the poorest students may not extend much beyond this basic list.

Reading Ability. The reading ability of any group of high school students also varies considerably. Dr. F. Wayne House tested 356 tenth-grade students enrolled in 15 different classes in six high schools in Columbus, Ohio. He found that they varied in reading ability "from a level comparable to the lowest 5 percent of seventh-grade students to a level comparable to the highest 5 percent of twelfth-grade students."

These three factors--intelligence, vocabulary, and reading ability--are probably the most significant ones in determining whether students are average, below average, or above average as far as their success in basic business classes is concerned.[1] By considering these factors and interpreting them in the light of

---

[1]It is understood, of course, that interest, family environment, memory, study skills, and reasoning ability are also important factors. For any given student any combination of selected factors may be the prime determinants in his standing in class.

the additional information the teacher has about his pupils, he can classify students accordingly.[2]

For the remainder of this discussion, those students who stand out above the "average" students will be referred to as superior students, and those who are below "average" will be called slow learners.[3]

WHAT ARE THE CHARACTERISTICS OF SUPERIOR STUDENTS?

Basic business teachers must learn to recognize superior students and develop activities that will challenge them to the maximum of their ability. The following characteristics distinguish superior students from other students.

Superior students read widely, have broad vocabularies, and possess a large fund of information. They delve readily into reference books for supplementary information and pursue periodical literature without being urged to do so.

Superior students are beyond their age norms in the maturity of their interests. Though their interests are wide, they may need deepening. They may need encouragement in delving deeper into topics of current interest. They are curious and ask many questions; they are eager to learn as much as they can and volun-

---

[2]A student whose IQ is approximately 100 (between 90 and 110), whose vocabulary is equal to that of the typical students in his class grade (using national norms), and whose reading level is within one grade of his classification would be an average student. It should be understood that a person who ranks slightly above the norms on one factor and slightly below on the others would be considered average.

[3]Carter V. Good, Ed., Dictionary of Education. 3rd ed. New York: McGraw-Hill, Inc., 1973. The author defines the slow-learning child as one "who exhibits slight intellectual retardation, requires adaptation of instruction and is slightly below average in learning ability."

teer for extra work. They are willing to undertake new tasks
and explore new areas of learning.

Superior students have good memories and long attention
spans. They possess creative imaginations; they can create
sketches for visual displays and write interesting dialogues for
plays and dramatic skits.

They are leaders and will accept responsibility readily.
They have the ability to direct the work of others and assist the
teacher in many ways in working with other students.

Perhaps the greatest degree of difference between superior
students and other students lies in their ability to grasp and
develop ideas. They can work with abstractions; they are good at
reflective thinking and problem solving. They possess good
reasoning abilities--they can define problems, analyze them, and
think them through, reaching logical conclusions. They enjoy
working with real problems.

HOW CAN TEACHERS PROVIDE FOR SUPERIOR STUDENTS?

Superior students should be held responsible for the best
work they can do. Because they can complete ordinary school
tasks without putting forth their maximum effort, they may develop poor work habits. To prevent this, basic business teachers
must challenge them through an enriched program of diversified
experiences suited to their broad interests and abilities.

Teachers should realize that the extra time available to
superior students must not be devoted to busy work or to additional endeavors of the same type as that already completed but
to new and challenging activities. Superior students can represent the school creditably in contacts with the business community, such as conducting surveys, arranging for field trips,
etc. They also possess the ability to evaluate films and supplementary reading materials and in other ways serve as teacher

aides. By utilizing their abilities in these ways, the teacher is not exploiting them. Rather, these experiences provide learning opportunities that enable students to develop abilities not afforded by the performance of the usual student activites.

Basic business classes are rich in opportunities for meeting the needs of superior students. Teachers need only to plan for them and give direction and purpose to their pursuits. The following activities represent ways and means of challenging students who have the time and inclination to go beyond the common learnings of the class as a whole. These are activities that superior students can engage in creditably and profitably.

Activities in Oral and Written Expression

1. Compose and write letters to foundations, commissions, chambers of commerce, and business firms for free materials pertinent to topics that are to be studied in the future.

2. Give class reports on articles in periodicals, pamphlets, and booklets that supplement and complement the textbook.

3. Serve as reporters for the class and perhaps the business department for the school newspaper.

4. Conduct research projects and prepare written reports of their findings.

5. Make individual or small-group field trips and report observations to the class.

6. Prepare a bibliography for a given topic based on reference materials available in the school library.

Creative Writing Activities

1. Serve as editors of a classroom newssheet calling attention to local events and radio and TV programs pertaining to business and current articles in business periodicals in the school library.

2. Prepare scripts for class dramatizations.

3. Plan a program to be given by the class in a school-wide assembly.

4. Plan a mock broadcast or telecast to be given as a special presentation in class.

Activities Associated with Visual Aids

1. Plan and prepare charts, graphs, and posters for class use.

2. Collect, classify, and file pictures suitable for reports, posters, and bulletin-board displays.

3. Preview films and filmstrips and evaluate them as to their suitability for class use.

4. Take pictures from which colored slides may be prepared for use in connection with oral reports to be given in class.

Coordinating and Supervisory Activities

1. Supervise a reading table supplied with supplementary booklets, pamphlets, and periodicals, keeping the material current and orderly.

2. Select from the school library books related to the topic being studied and arrange them on a special reference shelf in the classroom.

3. Contact businessmen who might serve as visiting speakers and orient them for their class appearance.

4. Survey the business community for suitable class field trips and take charge of the arrangement details.

5. Serve as teacher aides, guiding committee activities, explaining material to slow students, and guiding review sessions for small groups.

WHAT ARE THE CHARACTERISTICS OF SLOW LEARNERS?

Slow learners are weak in fundamental skills, in study skills, and in their basic drives and urges. They are less mentally mature than the majority of students in their grade and unable to deal adequately with most problems involving reflective thinking processes.

Fundamental Skills

Almost invariably, slow learners are weak in the fundamental skills. They are below average in both oral and written expression. Their vocabularies are inadequate: in the number of words they know, their ability to spell, and their preciseness in word choice and in word relationships. When they are reciting in class or replying to questions, their statements are usually brief and frequently lacking in clarity.

Their reading rates and comprehension levels are below those of the average students. Slow learners are probably two to four school grades behind the rest of the class in reading level. They are likely to need assistance in reading and understanding their textbooks and must be supplied supplementary printed materials that are well illustrated with visuals and written on a reading level below that of their grade in school.

Slow learners are inaccurate in simple computational skills and have great difficulty with the so-called written problems.

They are not alert observers. They fail to notice many things that happen around them that are observed by the better students in the class.

Study Skills

Slow learners almost always have poor study skills. They do not have a study schedule but choose more or less at random what

they are to study first. They do not plan ahead to make sure that
some time is allocated to each task to be done. In addition to
poor study mechanics, they do not get the maximum from the books
they read. They neither utilize library resources to a very great
degree nor do they use them effectively.

When they prepare for an examination, they are handicapped
because they have not prepared thorough outlines or systematic
sets of notes. They are unable to sort out the most important
ideas for study and review. When taking tests, they usually do
not reread their papers, proofreading for errors in spelling and
grammar and verifying their solutions. In addition to lacking
comprehensiveness, their answers generally are not well organized.

Basic Drives

Slow learners are dilatory about commencing their work. They
can find many things to consume time and delay studying, such as
sharpening and resharpening pencils, borrowing paper, searching
among the things in their desks for a pen or ruler, thumbing
through their texts or workbooks instead of using the table of
contents, etc. They quit easily and early. They must be pushed
to begin, held to the task, and encouraged to finish. They need
short-term goals, as well as intermediate and long-term objectives.
They do not plan for reviews but must be directed to review and
assisted in carrying through.

Mental Abilities

Slow learners are less mentally mature than the average of
their group. Their IQ's are low average or below; their memories
are short lived; and their attention spans are short. They are
poor at seeing relationships between words and ideas.

If asked to name all the objects they can see from where they sit, they name them at random rather than in related groups. For example, they may jump from ceiling to trees to walls, switch to people, and then jump back to grass. In contrast, superior students would name all parts of the room--walls, ceiling, floor, windows--and then move to another category, such as objects out of doors.

Slow learners are weak in rationalization, reflective thinking, and problem solving. They do not seek out the many applications of a rule or principle. They cannot detect inconsistencies in varying points of view or the errors in an illogical analysis. They are not able to handle abstract ideas.

When taking examinations, they do not plan their method of attack. They neither attempt the hard questions first to get them out of the way, nor do they read the group of questions over to select the ones they know best. They do not outline and organize a planned response. Rather, they take the questions in the order they appear and simply plunge in, writing "something" about each question.

Positive Attributes

On the positive side slow learners are usually near normal in sensory and motor abilities. While abstract ideas are beyond them, they learn well when working with concrete objects--things that they can see, feel, and handle. They may not use good judgment when selecting pictures to illustrate a given idea or principle. They may not be able to develop ideas for headings and subheadings for a bulletin board exhibit. But under the guidance and direction of the teacher, or a good student, they can carry through capably the mechanics of making a good exhibit. They may even have a superior sense of color harmony, balance, and arrangement. They may be accurate typists and be able to handle well the mechanics of duplicating the committee reports that are to be distributed to the class.

Slow learners usually accept responsibility willingly for routine tasks. They can keep the materials on a reading table neat and orderly. They are pleased to go to the film center to pick up films, operate and care for the projector, and serve as custodians of supplies and instructional materials.

Students Mistaken for Slow Learners

Young people of average or above average ability whose progress is impeded by unrecognized physical or emotional problems are sometimes mistaken for slow learners. Naturally, teachers should be aware of this possibility and be continually alert in an effort to detect such instances. Still other youngsters may be overly shy, may be slow in maturing, or may come from deprived homes. The school guidance counselors can be of service to basic business teachers here. When the special needs of these students are met, they will begin to live up to their potentialities.

HOW CAN TEACHERS PROVIDE FOR SLOW LEARNERS?

Slow learners should be helped to achieve the best work of which they are capable. Because they are weak in verbal activities, teachers should be careful to use simple language when explaining principles and to use numerous illustrations. When the teacher makes assignments, he should write them out whenever it is feasible to do so, and his instructions accompanying the assignments should be kept short. Examples may be used to supplement directions regarding assignments in some instances.

Since slow learners are not self-starters, teachers must give them a push. This may be done by following a discussion session with a supervised study period. During this time teachers should assist them in getting under way with their work. Another method is to give the slow students some special guidance at the beginning of a laboratory session. When a particular type of study procedure is being used for the first time, teachers might work through the first two or three items with the slow learners as a group.

Because slow learners have short attention spans and are not persistent in seeing projects through to completion, they should be given short assignments and projects that may be completed before interest wanes too greatly. Guidelines and mileposts are also helpful in keeping them abreast of their progress and keeping them up with their work. Teachers should see that a variety of tasks are undertaken within a class period.

Since slow learners do not plan their own reviews well, teachers may supply them with lists of questions, review sheets, and trial tests. In addition, review sessions may be planned for slow learners in small groups.

Because slow learners learn well through sensory experiences, teachers should make liberal use of various types of visuals: charts, graphs, slides, and motion pictures. Dramatizations and field trips are also especially helpful.

Experience with observable accomplishment is the key to success in the motivation of slow learners. So they should be led to compete with themselves (their own previous achievements) and not against others.

Following are some activities that slow learners may perform creditably in basic business classes:

Routine Classroom Activities

1. Serve on a committee performing receptionist functions for classroom visitors and outside speakers.

2. Serve as attendants for the room telephone.

3. Be responsible for attendance and other types of class records.

4. Act as monitors for distribution and collection of homework and supplementary materials.

Activities Assisting in Group Projects

1. Serve as typists for class reports and projects.
2. Construct models and displays for class or committees.
3. Help in duplicating reports and materials for class use.
4. Play simple roles in class dramatizations which do not
require a great deal of memorization.
5. Assist in survey activities by collecting and tabulating
data.

Activities Associated with Visual Aids

1. Set up audio-visual equipment, making it ready for class
use.
2. Act as projectionists for films and filmstrips.
3. Assist in preparing charts, graphs, and posters for class
use.
4. Serve as custodians of the reading table.
5. Be responsible for putting up bulletin-board exhibits.
6. Act as file clerks for instructional materials, such as
pictures and clippings.

HANDICAPPED STUDENTS

Basic business eduation is important to all students because
every individual functions as a consumer in the American economic
system. Consequently, students who have been classified as signi-
ficantly different intellectually and/or physically should be encouraged to take basic business courses. Because these students

have special characteristics, they may require special teaching methods or materials. Some basic teaching guidelines are presented here for three classifications of handicaps.

Visually Impaired

Students with acute sight deficiencies such as optic atrophy (frequent loss of clear vision), nystagmus (involuntary movement of the eyeballs), or loss of vision in one eye may find it difficult to read for long periods of time, thus reading assignments for these individuals should be kept at a minimum. More time should be allotted for written exams than is given the normally-sighted individual.

Some students are unable to differentiate colors. These students should not be required to interpret visuals if color is a factor necessary for understanding them.

Blind students may need to rely on tape-recorded classes and homework. Special equipment should be available on which teachers can record special instructions and evaluations of the students' work. Teachers should carefully explain all aspects of classroom demonstrations for students who cannot see.

If a student has been blind since birth, it is probable that he has learned to read Braille. A wide range of learning materials is available in Braille as well as on tape. The following organizations can provide assistance to teachers of visually handicapped students:

American Foundation for the Blind, Inc.
15 West Sixteenth Street
New York, NY 10011

Association for Education of the Visually Handicapped
919 Walnut Street
Philadelphia, PA 19107

Division for the Visually Handicapped
Council for Exceptional Children
1920 Association Drive
Reston, VA 22091

National Society for the Prevention of Blindness, Inc.
79 Madison Avenue
New York, NY 10016

Speech/Hearing Impaired

Students with a speech impairment may find class presentations difficult. If speaking embarrasses the students or if speech for extended periods is impossible, permit the speech-impaired students to write all reports. Encourage the students to participate in class discussion, however, and show patience and understanding when trying to understand the speech of extremely impaired students.

Hearing-impaired students should be seated near the teacher. This will increase the volume of the instruction for the hard-of-hearing students and allow non-hearing students an uninterrupted view of the teacher.

Teachers should be careful to face the class while speaking and to repeat the questions and comments made by students who are seated behind or distant from the hearing-impaired students. Intercom announcements should be repeated or written on the board.

Mentally Retarded

Mentally retarded students exhibit many of the characteristics of the slow learners but to a more extreme degree. It may be necessary to obtain lower grade level reading materials or video taped instruction for these students. Tests should be adapted to the vocabulary and reading level of the students, as well.

Teachers should be extremely patient with mentally retarded students--talking with them concretely, repeating information, making sure the students understand the material, and adjusting assignments to a comfortable learning level.

Teachers who have handicapped students in their classes should take special safety precautions. They should make certain that the students can maneuver about the classroom without injury to themselves or to others. They should also make special arrangements for these students in the event that evacuation from the building becomes necessary.

Teachers of handicapped students should contact their state's department of education to learn what special materials, or funds for the purchase of such materials, are available.

QUESTIONS, ACTIVITIES, AND PROJECTS

1. What are the different ways in which students differ one from another?

2. What are the characteristics of superior students?

3. Give some examples of ways to use projects to challenge superior students in basic business classes.

4. How may a teacher identify the slow learners in his classes?

5. What types of activities can slow learners perform most creditably in basic business classes?

6. In what ways may basic business teachers utilize superior students as teacher aides?

7. When setting up committees for special projects, would you group superior students together, average students together, and slow learners together or put superior, average, and slow learners all on the same committee? Why?

8. What types of teaching-learning activities seem to be equally effective with <u>both</u> <u>superior</u> <u>students</u> <u>and</u> <u>slow</u> <u>learners</u>?

9. Select a topic normally taught in an economics class and name specific activities you would suggest for the superior students in your class.

10. Select a topic normally taught in general business. Choose 8 or 10 important business terms used in a textbook discussion of the topic you have chosen. Prepare an assignment activity designed specifically to help the slow learners in your class to learn the meanings of the terms you have selected.

11. Design a game-type activity to be used when reviewing the topic of wise buymanship.

12. Utilizing your library, look up a formula which educators apply to text material to determine the reading level. Apply the formula to two high-school basic business texts.

CHAPTER 5

Dramatizing and Visualizing

Who doesn't enjoy a play? And who doesn't like a picture? Effective teachers of basic business subjects have mastered the techniques of presenting material dramatically, forcefully, and visually. Psychological studies indicate that students understand and retain as knowledge approximately one-tenth of the material they read, one-fifth of that which they hear, one-third of all they see, one-half of what they both hear and see, three-fourths of what they say, and nine-tenths of what they say and do. In this chapter ways and means of utilizing these very fine techniques in basic business classes are examined.

DRAMATIZING CLASS PRESENTATIONS

Almost anything that can be reported in monologue can be adapted to dramatic dialogue. Dramatic skits, brainstorming, and role playing are very effective teaching methods.

Rather than "tell" how to open a checking or savings account, why doesn't the teacher put on a skit? Instead of assigning a few pages to be read, why doesn't he auction off half of a dollar bill? The teacher should not "talk about" the importance of transportation; he should dramatize it!

For example, the teacher may set a breakfast table. He can assemble everything he needs at home in a few minutes--toaster, bread, eggs, cereal, milk, salt, pepper, a setting of china and silver, etc.--and bring them to class in a picnic basket. By asking where the various items on the table came from and how they got there, the teacher can illustrate clearly, graphically, and indelibly the importance of transportation in an economy built on specialization.

Rather than deliver a lecture on money as a medium of exchange, the teacher can stage a barter day. Holding up a ball point pen and announcing that on the following day he would like to trade it for something else, the teacher can ask the students to bring anything they like (in fact, several things) and say, "We shall have a barter day!" They will learn more about the need for money in a few minutes of trading than in an hour of listening. They will learn to appreciate the role that money plays in the exchange of goods and services.

For the usual textbook assignment, the teacher can substitute the following activity pertaining to the use of money substitutes. He can hold up for all to see a blank check and explain how it may be used for purchasing things. The students are asked to bring to class the following day something that may be used instead of money to buy articles in one or more of the local stores. The teacher offers a grade of $\underline{A}$ if no more than two students bring in the same money substitute, a grade of $\underline{B}$ if three persons bring the same item, and a grade of $\underline{C}$ if four or more have it.

Everyone will come to class with pockets bulging: money orders, traveler's checks, bank drafts, trading stamps, coupons, credit cards, bank notes, letters of credit, etc. Nothing will be in sight, and no student will volunteer at first. When called on to report, each student will proceed with caution, eyeing the others in the room to see if he alone is submitting his particular item. When the teacher asks how many other students have brought the money substitute being displayed, any response will come slowly and carefully. Only one other person will "show his hand" with that particular item because a third specimen would lower the grade for all three students to a B. There will be few students who do not make outstanding contributions.

USING VISUALS

The alert basic business teacher knows the real meaning of the Chinese proverb: "A picture is worth ten thousand words." When visual aids are used in teaching, students learn more and retain longer the things they learn. Visual materials, when utilized properly, enhance the building of concepts through observation when firsthand experiences are unavailable. They add interest and drama and stimulate thinking.

Visuals may be used to introduce a new topic by supplying background information. They may be used during the study of a topic for motivation, for clarification, or for demonstration. They may be used near the end of a unit for summary or review. Some visual aids may be used at all of these stages, emphasizing different things each time.

Visual aids and techniques of all types lend themselves well to the teaching of basic business. There are seven kinds of visuals that are commonly used: posters, bulletin boards, flannel boards, slides, transparencies, films or filmstrips, and video-tapes.

Posters

Posters are commonplace today--one cannot avoid them. One sees them in all types of stores, in window displays, and in busses and subway cars--they are used commercially to reach the consumer with an advertising message. They are used in hospitals and churches to communicate an idea or message to the casual observer or reader. They are used in schools for motivation and instruction. They must attract attention, hold it at least momentarily, and then get the message across quickly and convincingly. They must be colorful, simple, direct, and pleasing in appearance.

Many posters are available from businesses at little or no cost to the school, or the teacher may prepare his own posters. They may be prepared by and for the teacher or for student use. They may be prepared hurriedly for immediate one-time use only, or they may be prepared carefully and somewhat professionally for repeated use.

Mechanics of Making Posters. The following supplies for poster making should be kept in or near the classroom: paper or poster board (approximately 20 to 36 inches wide), a yardstick, rubber cement, felt writing pens and markers of varying colors, and a compartmented box containing a quantity of each letter of the alphabet in varying sizes and styles.

Posters made for repeated use should be well constructed-- prepared on stiff art board with precise lettering and ruling and brightened up with touches of color. Posters made for a temporary, immediate purpose--to perk interest, to enliven a learning situation, to summarize a committee report, or to illustrate a procedure or relationship--may be more simple. Their basic function is to crystallize class thinking and learning; they are used only once or twice.

One cannot justify students' spending a great deal of time making elaborate posters with painstaking lettering or art work. To the contrary, the paper used may be wrapping or ceiling paper; the lettering may be pasted on or hand-drawn with a broad-tipped poster pen or grease pencil. The illustrations may be pictures, hand-drawn charts or graphs, casual cutouts, or simple "stick figures."

The layout for each poster should be the responsibility of the student who prepares it. One of its principal values lies in deciding what it is to illustrate, what it should contain, and how it should be designed.

Bulletin-Board Exhibits

The bulletin board is a most effective visual display for use in basic business classes. It is a source of pleasure and pride to those who view it and a challenge to those who prepare it. The committee that prepares an exhibit should assume full responsibility for gathering together all the needed materials (pictures, letters, streamers, background paper, etc.) for developing its design and for posting it. All students, regardless of their ability level, can participate in preparing bulletin-board exhibits and get satisfaction and learning from the experience.

A bulletin-board exhibit sets the tone of a room, serves as a standard for neatness, and establishes a businesslike atmosphere. A glance at a classroom bulletin board gives an index to the personality of the teacher, his professional awareness, and the class achievement.

The honor of having one's work posted should be generously spread. Anyone can post the work of superior students, but it takes alertness and ingenuity to find something worth posting that is prepared by below-average students.

A Bulletin-Board Exhibit Should Have a Purpose. The bulletin board, like most other teaching aids, has a variety of uses, and its purpose must be kept in mind during its design and preparation. It should attempt to do only one thing. The teacher should ask himself: Is it to motivate? To introduce a topic for the first time? To show relationships between ideas already studied? Or to summarize, giving comprehensive coverage to the topic? Its purpose will determine to a great degree the scope of its contents.

Exhibits Must Be Easy to Interpret. The purpose of an exhibit is to make clear at a glance something that would otherwise require the use of many words. Therefore, the exhibit should be simple enough that the average observer can understand it. A caption at the top of the exhibit will tell what it is about. When in the form of a question, it draws special attention and encourages "a second look." In many cases, the main heading serves to give the exhibit balance and symmetry; it also serves as a theme, tying the display together. The lettering used should be legible, neat, and uniform in size and style. All headings and subheadings should be short, simple, and clear and should follow a uniform pattern.

Materials Used Should Be Accurate and Up-to-Date. If figures or statistics are to be included in exhibits, they should be accurate and current. Where graphs are shown, they should be accurately drawn and based on recent data; they should not reflect a situation that is no longer current. Pictures of equipment, for example, should be of recent models.

If a committee is preparing an exhibit pertaining to modern communication services, for example, the pictures used should include televisions, satellites used in world-wide telecasting, and automatic electronic equipment used for transmitting and receiving written communications, such as letters or telegrams. If modern transportation facilities are being depicted, the exhibit should include scenes such as the "piggy-back" operations of railroads, the use of huge cranes for loading entire boxcars into the holds of ships, and the use of conveyor belts for loading freight planes.

Good Mechanics Make Good Exhibits. There are many details regarding the building of bulletin-board exhibits that are important. They should be placed at eye level in a well lighted area in the flow of traffic. Color should be used to enhance the exhibits' power of attraction. It may be introduced into exhibits by using decorative paper for the backgrounds, by using ribbons as streamers leading from central objects to individual pictures in various positions in the exhibits, and by displaying colorful pictures. Border space should be provided at the sides of each exhibit as well as at the top and bottom.

Successive displays should be so strikingly different that the "steady trafficker" will realize that a new display has been posted.

Bulletin-Board Exhibits Should Be Prepared by Students. Preparing exhibits is a project that has universal interest and appeal to students. It gives rein to initiative and imagination, provides experience in organizing information, and gives meaning to class study. The class as a whole might suggest areas which lend themselves to bulletin-board displays. Then committees may be appointed to design and prepare the displays suggested. The committees may want to submit miniature sketches of their proposed designs for criticism before launching out on the real project. This refines the ideas to be illustrated and improves the quality of the final displays.

If any unusual materials are included, the source or person contributing them should be indicated. This may be written on a card giving the names of the committee members or on a separate card used just for this purpose.

Exhibits Should Be Changed Frequently. Occasionally one sees newspaper clippings that have turned yellow with age or that have dated headings which are months old displayed on bulletin boards as reports of "current" happenings. Sometimes the thumb tacks have fallen out, and the display material is hanging by only one corner.

Just as a placard advertising a play should be removed from store windows the day after the play has been given, bulletin-board exhibits should be removed as soon as their purposes have been adequately served. Most classrooms have only limited display areas, so materials must be removed to make room for new exhibits. As a general rule, bulletin-board exhibits should be left up for only a few days.

<u>The</u> <u>Teacher</u> <u>Should</u> <u>Maintain</u> <u>a</u> <u>Resource</u> <u>File</u>. The wise teacher will build up a file of display materials for use with the topics to be studied in the future. Many illustrations and pieces of art work can be used again next year. To be of greatest value, the materials should be arranged systematically and catalogued in such a way that it is easy to find what is being sought. Students are usually glad to assist in collecting and caring for materials for the resource file. They should have access to it for those "hard-to-get" items needed to complete their displays, after they have made an honest effort to find the pictures they need.

<u>The</u> <u>Flannel</u> <u>Board</u>

The flannel board can be the most colorful display used in basic business classes. Even among other attractive, eyecatching exhibits, it stands out. It is not a new teaching tool, but its use and effectiveness have been greatly underrated by many teachers.

The main feature of the flannel board is its simplicity. A piece of heavy cardboard, plywood, or wallboard is covered on one side with a sheet of flannel which is stretched tight and fastened securely.

How much one pays for the flannel seems to make little difference as long as it has a fluffy nap. Objects to be placed on it must have a flat surface, slightly roughened, that will cling to the flannel after the board is mounted on an easel. To make the objects cling, they may be backed with flannel, felt, a medium-grade sand paper, rough blotting paper, or suede paper.

The flannel board is a most versatile visual display; in addition to being colorful, it is most flexible. The teacher can use any design he wishes, building from left to right, from top to bottom, or from bottom to top. Most important of all is the fact that the teacher can build as he discusses--one point leading to another and each one illustrated in the exhibit.

The flannel board is not just a teacher's aid; it can be used as well by students when they present their class reports. Preparing the display pieces causes them to give serious thought to their reports, and using the flannel board makes the reports more interesting and dramatic.

Slides

Almost everything that has been said about posters, bulletin boards, and flannel boards may also be said of slides. By using almost any type of camera and color film for slides, photos may be taken of any display--poster, bulletin board, flip chart, or realia--and developed into 2 X 2 slides.

The slide projector is small, easy to carry and to store, and simple to operate--it is a most versatile teaching tool. Almost every topic to be taught in any basic business class may be illustrated through the use of slides.

For example, the services banks render may be illustrated with slides of the savings account window, the forms used (deposit slip, passbook, etc.) the safety-deposit vault, and a person being served by the loan department. Any person who knows how to use a camera and how to select the proper scenes can get all the pictures he needs in any local bank without having "poses" for any of them. For the unit on wise buymanship snaps may be made of advertisements (newspapers, billboards, window displays) and signs showing the discount available on canned goods if they are purchased in large quantities, etc.

Films and Filmstrips

Look, listen, and learn are the watch words when using educational films. Probably no other visual aid has a stronger appeal for secondary school youth.

The teacher is responsible for screening and selecting the film. He should always preview the film before showing it in class. Students should know why they are viewing it and what to look for. Films are effective only if there is some form of follow up. The principles discussed here apply to the use of both films and filmstrips.

Advantages of Using Films and Filmstrips. Although many high school students have traveled widely and experienced many things, most students have only limited observations and experiences in the world of business. Opportunities for taking entire class groups on field trips for direct observations are limited; therefore, educational films and filmstrips play perhaps their most important role by bringing scenes from business--scenes not available in the local community--into the classroom. Through these visual techniques students can observe, for example, how cars are made, what types of work are performed in business offices, or how the different means of communication may be utilized by individuals and businesses.

Films save time, for in a few minutes students can see in a film what would require hours to see firsthand. This is especially true when the scenes being shown are collected from widely separated places. A film or filmstrip can be introduced, observed, and discussed in a single class period, while it would require at least three different class periods to prepare for, conduct, and follow up a field trip experience. Also, in a film or filmstrip everyone can hear the commentator, whereas on many field trips only those near the guide can hear his explanations.

Before Showing the Film. The teacher should preview films before showing them in class. This enables him to tell the students what to look for as they watch it. Also, it is impossible to remember everything that a film covers. So while previewing it, the teacher can make notes on all the things to be discussed in class. In fact, it is a good idea for him to write out the questions he wants to ask. These questions occur to the teacher better during the previewing than at any other time. In the case of filmstrips, oftentimes the questions are stated right on the strip.

In some instances the teacher may decide that a class committee should preview the film or filmstrip before it is viewed by the entire class. He will want to decide how best to follow up the film or filmstrip with culminating student activities.

The teacher should be certain that the projector is reserved. If at all possible, the projector should be set up prior to the class period. The teacher should also be familiar with the complete operation of the film projector or should have someone who has such expertise present during the showing.

Viewing the Film. Classes should not be combined for a film showing. It should be a normal part of the classwork just like other class activities. When a film is an integral part of the work of a particular class, it is most meaningful to students. When two or more classes are combined and moved to a larger room for film showings, it takes on the atmosphere of a "movie" instead of an instructional film.

There are some guidelines that students should observe to get the maximum value from viewing films. Students should become familiar with these suggestions, and occasionally the teacher should review them with the class prior to showing a film. The suggestions are: Students should keep the film title in mind and watch the opening scenes for orientation to the film's setting, purposes, and content. They should not be concerned with hair or clothing styles but should watch for information, ideas, and examples. Since most students do not make notes during a film, they should peg important statements mentally so they can write things down after the showing is completed or ask questions for further clarification. They should look for and understand certain mechanical features film producers employ, including: a fade-in, fade-out, flashback, or summary statement, which indicates a transition point in the theme of the film; a chart, which gives statistical data; a graph, which presents a trend covering a period of time; and a shift to slow motion or a word caption at the top or bottom of a scene, which emphasizes key points.

After Seeing the Film. The discussion following the film is perhaps the most important part of all, for it determines the degree to which the students have understood and applied the information and ideas presented in the film. Class discussion ties together what the students have seen, helps them to interpret their observations on and the facts presented in the film, and increases the students' retention, or degree of learning, of the material.

It is frequently helpful to allow students a short period of time to make notes on what they have seen. Afterward they may be able to make their notes more complete as class discussion ensues. It is sometimes helpful if students are asked to write out one question that was raised in their minds while viewing the film. This practice also encourages students to raise questions during the showing and to give close attention when viewing films on future occasions.

An oral review of the main ideas contained in the film--given sometimes by the teacher but usually by a student--is always good. The student should be designated prior to the film showing so that he will be well prepared to speak. If it is a long film, more than one person may share this responsibility.

When the teacher previews the film, he should note items about which he will want to ask questions during the follow-up discussion after the showing. These questions serve several helpful purposes: they clarify difficult or unusual points or incidents in the film; they emphasize certain facts through repetition; and they encourage students to be alert when viewing films.

Many films briefly introduce topics or ideas that may later be explored more fully by individuals, committees, or the entire class. Various possible future activities should be discussed, specific explorations suggested, and assignments made by the teacher or accepted voluntarily by class members. It may be that the film should be shown again at some future date. If so, it should be decided when this is to be done, who is responsible for showing it, and who is to view it. It has been demonstrated that pupils learn about one-third more from a second showing of most films.

Sources of Information. Lists of films and/or filmstrips suitable for use in basic business classes may be obtained from the following sources:

AIMS Instructional Media, Inc.
626 Justin Avenue
Glendale, CA 91201

American Bankers Association
1120 Connecticut Avenue, NW
Washington, DC 20036

American Council of Life Insurance
277 Park Avenue
New York, NY 10017

Association-Sterling Films
600 Grand Avenue
Ridgefield, NJ 07657

Broadcasting Foundation of America
52 Vanderbilt Avenue
New York, NY 10017

Business Education Films
5113 Sixteenth Avenue
Brooklyn, NY 11204

Center for Humanities
Communications Park
Box 100
White Plains, NY 10602

Chamber of Commerce of the United States
Audio Visual Department
1615 H Street, NW
Washington, DC 20062

Household Finance Corporation
Prudential Plaza
Chicago, IL 60601

Joint Council on Economic Education
1212 Park Avenue
New York, NY 10036

McGraw-Hill Book Company
Text-Film Department
1221 Avenue of the Americas
New York, NY 10020

Modern Talking Picture Service
Film Scheduling Center
5000 Park Street, N
St. Petersburg, FL 33709

National Association of Manufacturers
Education Department
1776 F Street, NW
Washington, DC 20006

National Audio-Visual Center
National Archives Building
General Services Administration
Washington, DC 20409

Society for Visual Education
1345 Diversey Parkway
Chicago, IL 60614

Walter J. Klein Company
6301 Carmel Road
Charlotte, NC 28211

Overhead Transparencies

Overhead projectors and transparencies are frequently used
in the basic business classroom. They allow the teacher to control the use of a visual under normal lighting while facing the
students at the front of the room. The teacher can obtain professionally prepared transparencies and transparency masters from
numerous sources, or he can create custom-made transparencies.
The teacher should observe caution, however, in the selection,
creation, and use of transparencies.

A transparency, when projected on the screen at the front of
the room, should be visible to the student farthest from it.
Lettering can be done manually, with a special typewriter or a
special typewriter element, or with commercially prepared, rub-on
letters.

Writing on transparency film may be done easily and quickly with a felt-tipped pen made for such use. The writing done in this manner can be removed with a damp cloth, and the transparency film may then be reused.

Color can be added to the transparency through the use of colored transparency film or colored pens. It is recommended that the teacher use no more than two colors per transparency unless additional colors aid in understanding the material being presented.

The teachers should be careful not to block the projection by standing in front of the screen or by placing a hand over the material on the projector. If something specific is to be highlighted, it should be done with a pen at the projector.

A cardboard frame surrounding the transparency lengthens the life of the plastic film. Frames are also useful for recording special notes or teaching information relevant to the topic being illustrated.

Information can be taught in progressive stages through two methods which adapt easily to the overhead transparency. First, the teacher can present a list, one item at a time, by utilizing masks. These are strips of paper attached to the frame which cover each item of information but which can be folded back, revealing the items beneath them. If the list appears in order vertically, the teacher can simply cover the transparency with a sheet of paper and slide the paper down the transparency page, revealing one item at a time. The primary advantage of masking is that it allows the teacher to control the pace of the learning while it focuses attention on the item being discussed.

The second method is the overlay. Transparencies can be stacked, one over the other, allowing the teacher to add information progressively. This method is especially helpful with pictures which are complex. One feature can be presented and discussed, and the others can be added one at a time until the

picture is complete. To insure accurate alignment of the over-
lays, the teacher should attach them to the frame.

Video Tape Recordings

The video tape recorder is available in many high schools.
It is easy to operate and has several uses in basic business
classrooms.

When field trips are difficult to arrange because of
scheduling and/or transportation problems, for example, the
teacher can bring the experience to the classroom by video taping
an individual's or committee's tour of a business.

The teacher can also bring guest speakers and special events
to the classroom through the use of video tape recordings.

Students can use the video tape recorder to tape mock job
interviews. Frequently the students can spot their mistakes and
correct them more easily if they are allowed to critique their
own performances.

Utilization of a video tape recorder which attaches to a
television set enables the teacher to record television shows or
segments of shows which might be used in the classroom. This
includes shows such as investigative news programs and consumer-
tip broadcasts.

QUESTIONS, ACTIVITIES, AND PROJECTS

1. What are the characteristics of a good bulletin-board
    exhibit?
2. How can a teacher make sure that students understand the
    purpose of a poster or bulletin-board display?
3. What values accrue to students from their participation in
    the preparation of posters and bulletin-board exhibits?
4. What advantages does a flannel board have over other types
    of visuals?

5. What criteria would you use in selecting a film for use in a basic business class?

6. How would you prepare a class to view a film?

7. After your class has viewed a film, what procedure would you use to reinforce the concepts it attempts to teach?

8. Prepare a poster or bulletin-board exhibit for use in consumer economics or business law.

9. Prepare a flexible flannel board. Obtain a piece of flannel, approximately 30 by 36 inches, and hem the two ends so that rods (aluminum or steel may be used) may be inserted in them. This flannel board can be used with any portable tack board just by letting the heavier rod fall over the top of the tack board and hang down a few inches from the top on the back side. This weight supports the flannel, and the lighter rod at the bottom holds it tight.

10. Take pictures to illustrate different aspects of some topic, such as production, distribution, banking, advertising, savings, or insurance. Prepare the pictures or slides for use in your classes.

CHAPTER 6

Teacher Planning for Basic
Business Subjects

Who would undertake to build an important building or bridge
without an adequate set of blueprints? What teacher would undertake the important task of teaching without a lesson plan?

There is a strong similarity between the work of a builder
and that of a teacher--coordination. The chief function of a
general contractor is to coordinate and supervise the work of the
subcontractors--those who actually construct the building. The
teacher's chief role is to guide, coordinate, and supervise the
work of the "subcontractors" in the classroom--the individuals,
the committees, and the groups that put the total learning experience together.

The work of building subcontractors is interrelated--no one
works in a vacuum. Similarly, there are many ways in which the
tasks of individuals, committees, and groups in basic business
classes are intertwined and interdependent. No student works in
complete isolation.

The subject matter and the experiences of the students are
related. One does not teach bits of information for subject
matter's sake but emphasizes interpreting information, reflective
thinking, and problem solving. What one learns tomorrow is greatly
affected by the learning which takes place today.

The analogy between the work of a building contractor and that of a teacher has been drawn to emphasize the importance of planning and the significance of guiding, coordinating, and supervising in the classroom. However, there is a very significant difference between the functions of the two that must be emphasized at this point. The work of the building contractor is "fixed"--it must follow the blueprints. In contrast, the work of the teacher-coordinator and his student "subcontractors" is most flexible--the activities and subject matter change and develop as the group proceeds with its study of a unit topic. In fact, the terms "flexibility" and "cooperative student-teacher action" might be said to be the key theses of unit planning.

WHAT IS UNIT TEACHING?

The unit method of teaching is a result of fusing and integrating students' learning into a whole. When students and teachers set up problems together and work cooperatively to solve those problems, a good learning situation exists. When the students' objectives are in agreement with the teacher's objectives, when the teacher's goals are as interesting and as acceptable as the students', and when the students' goals are as worthy as the teacher's, learning always takes place.

Harold B. Alberty emphasizes one of the basic criteria of true cooperative effort when he states:

> Effective student participation in the high school is contingent on the creation of a democratic climate for learning and an understanding of group processes in the classroom.
>
> The school sensitive to its democratic commitment, therefore, seeks to develop the ability to examine authorities critically and to give allegiance to policies and programs which further the social goals of our society. Students, must, therefore, have a voice in

90

planning and carrying into effect the activities which make up the school program. In
this manner they learn through the actual
processes of living that certain ways of behaving defeat the realization of the goals
which they helped to establish, and that
other ways of behaving promote the attainment of these goals. . . . behavior being
<u>directed</u> <u>by</u> <u>the</u> <u>teacher</u> toward the develop-
ment of individuals who assume responsibility
for their own conduct. . . .[1]

Factors which make a unit topic desirable are (1) value for
students, now and/or later, (2) breadth sufficient for many to
work on it, (3) interest of the group in the topic, and (4)
availability of materials for the topic.

The important steps in democratic unit teaching are:

1. Taking a preliminary survey of students' backgrounds
   and needs.

2. Setting up the criteria for choosing worthwhile group
   experiences.

3. Examining a range of possible worthwhile group
   activities.

4. Choosing cooperatively the best possible experiences.

5. Caring for the rights of the minority.

6. Assigning tasks to complete student experiences.

7. Revising the group's working plans as needs dictate.

8. Evaluating the group's work upon completion of the
   group experience or unit.

Here's the Way It Works

The best way to answer students' questions about the way
goods are produced is to visit a factory and let the students ask

---

[1]Harold B. Alberty and Elsie J. Albert, <u>Reorganizing the
High-School Curriculum</u>. Third ed. New York: The Macmillan Co.,
1962, pp. 341-343.

questions of their guide as they go through. They will leave the plant with knowledge they didn't have before; they will be enthusiastic and interested and will have a desire to learn more about production.

The teacher provides the necessary guidance, serving as a consultant and resource person. He encourages students to ask questions and suggests other questions that have not occurred to them. He suggests books, bulletins, periodical references, and motion pictures that help answer these questions, and he helps students locate them. Students and teacher work together in researching, making notes, and writing summaries of what they have learned. Together they decide what committees are necessary and who is to be on each committee. Cooperatively, they decide on the methods to use in sharing their findings--reports, dramatizations, exhibits, etc.

It may develop that a small committee needs to return to the factory and interview the foreman. This introduces the new problem of preparing for and conducting interviews. (If this is the first time that the problem of interviews has arisen, it would be wise to take time to pursue this problem, even to the point of practicing mock interviews.) A chief concern in unit teaching is to make the learning as real as possible.

OUTLINE FOR PLANNING UNITS

The various phases of unit planning are:

1. Identification
    a. Title of the unit.
    b. Justification of the unit, foreword, or overview.

2. Objectives--the goals to be accomplished in studying the unit. (Omit those which are common to other units, such as the development of desirable attitudes and good citizenship or the improvement of study skills.)

3. <u>Scope</u> <u>and</u> <u>Content</u>
   a. Outline of the content of the unit topic.
   b. Main subdivisions and how they are related.
   c. Boundaries or limits of the problem area.
   d. Important issues, concepts, and problems in the unit topic.

4. <u>Launching</u> <u>the</u> <u>Unit</u>--how it is to be introduced.

5. <u>Suggested</u> <u>Student</u> <u>Activities</u>--individual and group.
   a. Important things students might want to know and do.
   b. Committees that might be appointed and what they might do.

6. <u>Visual</u> <u>Materials</u> <u>and</u> <u>Motivation</u> <u>Devices</u>
   a. Specific visual materials to use--pictures, charts, graphs, posters, bulletin boards, flannel-board presentations, films, filmstrips.
   b. Ways to spice the unit and stimulate interest--oral reports, panels, demonstrations, dramatizations, interviews, observations, excursions, speakers.

7. <u>Reference</u> <u>Materials</u>
   a. Resource materials for teacher use.
   b. Resource materials for student use.

8. <u>Evaluation</u>
   a. How students are to evaluate their work.
   b. How the teacher is to evaluate the students' work.

Unit teaching must be flexible--it grows as it goes. Though the teacher has thought through all of these plans, he does not follow a "cut-and-dried" procedure. He lets things develop as he and the class work and study together. But because of his prior planning he knows what the possibilities are and is ready to suggest activities and resource materials when the need arises and the opportunity occurs.

<u>Some Specifics in Planning</u>

There are two types of planning for any unit. The teacher plans before the unit starts; then the teacher and the students plan together. The steps involved in these five types of planning are as follows:

1. <u>Before the unit starts, the teacher</u>:
   a. Develops objectives of the unit study.
   b. Gathers supplementary books and pamphlets.
   c. Scans the material collected and prepares a tentative outline of subject matter content.
   d. Prepares a bibliography.
   e. Decides on some concepts he hopes students will develop.
   f. Prepares a vocabulary list of new and important terms.
   g. Decides tentatively on some possible student activities and experiences.
   h. Decides on the way to approach or introduce the topic.
2. <u>Together the teacher and students</u>:
   a. Explore the new unit topic in the approach.
   b. Decide on some problems to solve and items to investigate.
   c. Set up committee or group projects.
   d. Decide upon plans of action to achieve objectives.
   e. Plan culminating and evaluation procedures.

WAYS TO INTRODUCE A UNIT OF WORK

There are many ways to begin a unit study. Most topics may be launched in several different ways. Therefore, teachers utilize different methods, thus giving variety to classroom work. The following are approaches to new unit topics that are especially suited to the content of basic business classes:

Methods Utilizing Visual Aids

1. Films or filmstrips
2. Slides
3. Bulletin boards or flannel boards
4. Collections of still pictures or photographs

Methods Which Are Student Centered

1. Dramatic skits or role playing
2. Demonstrations
3. Oral reports
4. Panel or group discussions
5. Accounts of personal experiences
6. Field trips or field trip reports
7. Local happenings involving students
8. Reports of interviews

Methods Which Are Teacher Centered

1. Case stories or illustrations
2. Case problems
3. Series of questions
4. Pretests
5. Guest speaker
6. Overview presentation
7. Report of newspaper story or magazine article

VALUES OF UNIT TEACHING

The most important value of unit teaching is that it takes the tension out of the class situation by integrating learning activities into a unit or whole.

A second value is that it helps meet individual differences. This is true because it utilizes committee and group projects enabling students to undertake work in line with their individual capacities.

A third value of unit teaching is that it capitalizes on the natural ways that people learn: by asking questions, by observing, and by experiencing firsthand.

The most lasting values of unit teaching are sometimes called the "plus" values; not only do students learn facts, but also they learn give-and-take, tolerance, courtesy, consideration of others, and other skills necessary for living and working happily together.

UTILIZING RESOURCE MATERIALS

Dynamic teachers of basic business subjects enrich their teaching through the continual use of current resource material. There is quite a variety of types and sources of both printed and visual aids. A discussion of some of the leading sources is included here.

Publishers' Supplementary Aids

Today's textbooks are supplemented by study guides for the students and suggestion manuals for the teacher. Study guides usually review new terminology, furnish forms for completing assignments from the textbooks, offer supplementary assignments, and supply objective test items as an aid in reviewing the content of the textbooks.

The teacher's manuals include: answers to textbook questions and problems; ways to introduce unit topics; suggestions for student and committee activities; ideas for posters, bulletin-board exhibits, and overhead transparencies; and titles of recommended films and filmstrips.

Many practice sets, case study booklets, and other such supplementary teaching materials are also available from textbook publishers.

Yearbooks of Professional Associations

Both regional and national associations publish yearbooks which are supplied to their members. The overall theme of the yearbook is changed each year, but as a general rule, a major section of the yearbook is devoted to the different subject-matter areas. Almost every yearbook contains one or more chapters dealing with various aspects of teaching the various basic business subjects. Occasionally an entire yearbook is devoted in large measure or exclusively to the teaching of the basic business subjects.

Paperback Books

Numerous books that are especially good for supplementary reading by the best students in basic business classes are continually being published as paperbacks. They are excellent reading for basic business teachers, too.

Professional Periodicals

The professional magazines regularly carry articles dealing with teaching the basic business subjects. Some of these are general discussions but others deal with specific subject matter topics. Each year, the Business Education Forum features articles pertaining to teaching basic business subjects. The titles and publishers of these periodicals, which are published monthly or bimonthly, are:

> The Balance Sheet, published by
> South-Western Publishing Company
> 5101 Madison Road
> Cincinnati, OH 45227
> (free to school address)

Business Education Forum, published by:

> National Business Education Association
> 1906 Associate Drive
> Reston, VA 22091
> (free to association members)

Business Education World, published by:

> Gregg Division and Community College Division
> McGraw-Hill Book Company
> 1221 Avenue of the Americas
> New York, NY 10036
> (free to school address)

Delta Pi Epsilon Journal, published by:

> Delta Pi Epsilon
> Ellis J. Jones, Executive Secretary
> Gustavus Adolphus College
> St. Peter, MN 56082
> (free to members)

Journal of Business Education, published by:

> Heldref Publications
> 4000 Albermarle Street, NW
> Washington, DC 20016

Journal of Consumer Affairs, published by:

> University of Missouri
> 162 Stanley Hall
> Columbia, MO 65201

Pamphlets, Bulletins, and Booklets

A number of business organizations publish helpful teaching aids that are especially useful in basic business classes. Catalogues and published lists of their available materials will be sent on request. The names and addresses of selected organizations, associations, and institutes are given here. (In addition to printed materials, several of these also have filmstrips which may be borrowed or purchased.)

> American Bankers Association
> 1120 Connecticut Avenue, NW
> Washington, DC 20036

American Stock Exchange
86 Trinity Place
New York, NY 10006

Associated Credit Bureaus, Inc.
6767 Southwest Freeway
Houston, TX 77074

Association of Stock Exchange Firms
24 Broad Street
New York, NY 10024

Automobile Manufacturers Association
320 New Center Building
Detroit, MI 48202

Chamber of Commerce of the United States
1615 H Street, NW
Washington, DC 20062

Council of Better Business Bureaus, Inc.
1150 17th Street, NW
Washington, DC 20036

Federal Reserve System
Public Services
Washington, DC 20551

Federal Trade Commission
6th Street and Pennsylvania Avenue, NW
Washington, DC 20580

Ford Motor Company
3000 Schaefer Road
Dearborn, MI 48126

General Motors Corporation
Department of Public Relations
Detroit, MI 48202

Household Finance Corporation
Consumer Education Department
Prudential Building
Chicago, IL 60601

Institute of Life Insurance
Educational Division
277 Park Avenue
New York, NY 10017

Insurance Information Institute
110 William Street
New York, NY 10038

Joint Council on Economic Education
1212 Park Avenue
New York, NY 10036

Merrill Lynch, Pierce, Fenner & Smith, Inc.
One Liberty Plaza
New York, NY 10006

National Association of Manufacturers
Education Department
1776 F Street, NW
Washington, DC 20006

National Consumer Finance Association
1000 Sixteenth Street, NW
Washington, DC 20036

New York Stock Exchange
11 Wall Street
New York, NY 10005

U.S. Government Printing Office
Superintendent of Documents
Washington, DC 20402

Reference Periodicals

Several periodicals regularly include numerous articles that serve as current supplementary material for basic business teachers. They are as follows:

Business Week, published by:
  McGraw-Hill Book Company
  1221 Avenue of the Americas
  New York, NY 10036

Changing Times, published by:
  Kiplinger Editors
  Editors Park, MD 20782

Consumer Reports, published by:
  Consumers Union
  256 Washington Street
  Mount Vernon, NY 10550

Forbes, published by:
  Forbes, Inc.
  60 Fifth Avenue
  New York, NY 10011

Fortune, published by:

Time, Inc.
541 N. Fairbanks Court
Chicago, IL 60611

Nation's Business, published by:

Chamber of Commerce of the United States
1615 H Street, NW
Washington, DC 20006

U.S. News & World Report, published by:

U.S. News & World Report
2300 N Street, NW
Washington, DC 20037

Selecting and Evaluating Resource Materials

The teacher is responsible for evaluating the reading level of his students and selecting resource materials that are appropriate for use in his class. In order to do this effectively some type of criterion or checklist should be utilized. One such checklist, which appeared in the EBTA Yearbook, "Social-Business Economic Education," follows:

Physiognomy
1. Is the resource material immediately attractive and appealing?
2. Are the size, shape, and weight of the material suitable for the purpose?
3. Are the style and size of type clear and suitable for the ability and interest levels of the readers?
4. Are the weight and finish of the binding and inside pages appropriate for the purpose?
5. Is the material free from obtrusive advertising?

Style of Writing
6. Is the writing style interesting and does it stimulate curiosity and imagination?
7. Is the vocabulary on the level of ability and interest of the readers?

8. Is the writing clear and readable?

9. Is there a logical development of ideas?

Arrangement and Organization of Content

10. Does the material have an interesting and logical format?

11. Is there sufficient content for the purpose?

12. Is there coverage of the areas of content desired?

13. Does the material add to the information already on hand?

14. Are the contents organized in a psychologically sound manner to facilitate teaching?

15. Are there sufficient illustrations, explanations, and visual presentations?

16. Is provision made for individual differences of the students' needs and abilities in the length and depth of exercises to be completed?

17. Is there a variety of exercises to be completed?

18. Are there sufficient reviews and summaries to help synthesize the content?

19. Are sufficient supplementary materials available?

Content

20. Is the content accurate and authentic?

21. Is the content factual, unbiased, and free from exaggeration?

22. Is the content timely and up-to-date?

23. Is the content relevant to the purpose?

24. Is the content meaningful and interesting?

25. Is the content comprehensive?

Authorship

26. Has the author had sufficient education and experience to be competent in the area?

27. Does the author allow proprietary interests to distort the truth?

Usefulness

28. Does the material meet the user's objectives?

29. Is the value of the material worth its cost in time and money?

30. Is there time to utilize the material sufficiently to justify its cost in time and money?

31. Can the same information be obtained elsewhere with less expenditure of time, money, and effort?

32. Will the material duplicate what is already known or on hand?

In Chapter 10 are many helpful ideas for teaching selected topics which are included in general business, business law, economics, and consumer economics courses.

QUESTIONS, ACTIVITIES, AND PROJECTS

1. After you have developed the content outline for a resource unit, what would most logically be your next step?

2. What two ways of launching unit topics are your favorites?

3. Explain the meaning of this statement: "Flexibility and cooperative student-teacher action are key theses in unit teaching."

4. Assume you wish to have your economics class study some specific topic. What criteria would you use in deciding whether the topic is appropriate?

5. How valuable is teacher time spent in planning versus time spent in evaluating?

6. Assume that you plan to use a resource person from government in connection with your class study of taxes. Where specifically would you seek such a resource person?

7. Select a unit topic normally taught in both general business and consumer economics. Develop for the topic:
   a. Objectives
   b. A content outline
   c. Suggestions for launching the unit
   d. Suggestions for student activities
   e. Suggestions for "spicing" student interest

8. Select a supplementary booklet suitable for use in an economics class. Evaluate it, using the checklist taken from the EBTA Yearbook and reproduced in this chapter.

9. Select a topic normally taught in general business and prepare a "pretest" for use in launching the topic.

10. Select a high school basic business text and, utilizing a
    local high school's calendar, prepare a year plan, choosing
    the most effective sequence and time of year for the units
    to be taught.

*A smart person is not one who knows
all of the answers, but one who has the
ability to determine all of the answers.*

CHAPTER 7

Teaching for Concept Development
and Problem Solving

One of the highest goals in teaching is to help students develop competence in making decisions. Another is to guide them as they become worthy citizens in the democratic way of life. These goals may be achieved best through teaching for concept development and problem solving.

Students must practice analyzing problems and breaking them into meaningful interrelationships. They must reach their own conclusions as they face the facts of everyday living. Students must learn the application of facts as well as the facts themselves. Therefore, teachers must give students guidance and set up meaningful problem situations for them to solve, while permitting them to seek out and discover their own answers. They may work individually or in small groups.

This method requires more time than merely mastering facts per se. But students respond to the challenge of it, bring more interest to class, participate more freely, and utilize supplementary materials to a greater degree. They feel "free" and "safe" in the learning situation, and the results obtained are more important and longer lasting.

The ability to approach problem solving scientifically is of considerably greater value to the individual than the ability to

remember facts. Specific learnings about social security, labor
unions, and government may become outdated within a single decade,
but the use of a logical, organized approach to problem solving
can be adapted to new situations. When students are permitted to
approach learning as a task of discovering something rather than
"reading about it," they receive a reward that can never come
from just memorizing factual information. This reward, which
comes from honest inquiry, is observable growth in their competency
in finding solutions to problems.

The study of basic business subjects affords students abun-
dant opportunities to practice decision making relative to present
and future business problems. Students must learn to interpret
fundamental business data and develop broad meaningful concepts
that are not readily forgotten. Teachers must set up pseudo and
real problem situations that require students to reach decisions
and to defend them.

To obtain maximum benefit from problem solving, every possible effort should be made to utilize the local community as a
laboratory. Actual happenings in the business life of any community are reported regularly in the local newspapers. The teacher must know the resources available in his community and develop
suitable problems and projects for investigation and study. Most
business and governmental organizations will cooperate fully and
enthusiastically with teachers. Many ideas for class problems
and projects can be found in current professional business education journals.

CONCEPT DEVELOPMENT

A concept is "a mental image of a thing formed by generaliza-
tion from particulars--an idea of what a thing in general should

be."[1] This means that it is a thought or opinion derived from an interpretation of facts. The concept developed will be determined by the accuracy and completeness of the facts as well as the reliability and truthfulness of the generalizing done by the students.

Students must be motivated to apply the facts they learn in their personal everyday activities. What value is there in learning that a good investment must be safe, must yield an acceptable return, and must be available when needed, if this is merely memorized or learned theoretically? Since students' interests, knowledge, experience, backgrounds, and situations all vary, all students must formulate their own generalizations. Students need to broaden their thinking by working from specifics to general principles. The teacher's responsibility is to encourage, guide, coordinate, and supervise the individual and group projects. The teacher must remember that sound concepts are formulated only when accurate and appropriate specifics are applied. The more specific the concept is and the closer it is related to the facts on which it is based, the easier it is to develop.

THE PROBLEM SOLVING PROCESS

Concept development and problem solving are quite similar and follow almost identical steps. The first essentials to problem solving are (1) the recognition that a problem exists and (2) the presence of a desire to find its solution.

The Formal Steps or Procedures

1. The first step is to state the problem clearly and separate it into various aspects and subproblems. This helps to get

---

[1]From Webster's New Collegiate Dictionary.

the problem in mind and understand what is needed to get started. For example, the problem is: How does one go about choosing an insurance agent? The subproblems are: What are the qualifications of a good agent? How does one locate a good agent? Whose recommendations should one accept? How can an individual tell whether a particular agent is the right one for him?

2. The second step is to determine what is already known about the problem. Before one starts looking for new facts, he should first exhaust his present knowledge of the general problem and its component parts.

3. The third step is to decide what new knowledge is needed and to gather new facts. These are not bits of information to be learned for their own sake but to be used because of their bearing upon the problem at hand. As was previously stated, concepts are based on facts.

4. The fourth step is to sort through the facts and assimilate them to find their interrelationships. A study of the interrelationships of relevant facts leads to a clear perception and knowledge of significant truths.

When studying life insurance, for example, a student learns that there are different kinds of policies--straight life, limited payment, term, etc.--and that they vary from one another in their basic features, uses, and cost. Only by relating these bits of information to one another and to the problem as a whole does the student realize that there are policies available to meet widely varying individual needs and circumstances. By assimilating related knowledge he gains an understanding of the problem and is in a position to seek its solution.

5. The fifth step is to interpret and reflect upon relationships and to seek plausible solutions. At this stage students search for ideas, reason from facts that now have meaning for them, put related facts together to formulate concepts, and reach conclusions.

For example, the students learn that they spread the costs of a risk over a period of years by sharing the risk with others through life insurance; that they create an estate for themselves and their families by paying their first premiums; that different types of policies meet varying needs; that these needs will vary from time to time; and that young people cannot afford during their early work years all the protection they and their families will ultimately need.

Students generalize by putting all of these interrelated learnings together and reach several conclusions. They first conclude that buying life insurance is an important and integral part of their overall financial planning. They also conclude that buying life insurance is not a one-time operation but something that should be planned and reprogrammed from time to time. The students conclude that they need the help and guidance of an insurance agent who has made a detailed study of the topic and that they should choose an agent of experience--one who has had contact with many problems similar to theirs and one who will be available during the years ahead. All of these generalizations are based upon specific facts which are related to one another and are properly interpreted in light of a person's understanding of a problem and its various components--a problem that is important to the individual personally and needs to be solved.

6. The sixth step is to test conclusions and solutions and choose the one or ones that seem best under the circumstances. Actually, the example poses a double problem. The first is the actual choice of insurance coverage and the determination of the amount to purchase. The intermediate problem is the choice of an agent to help in making the former decision. One's banker and one's business associates (or those of one's parents) can suggest the names of insurance agents of experience and good reputation. But among them is the best agent for a particular person. By choosing an agent and talking with that agent, one can tell whether

the agent is suitable. Thus, one tests the decisions he has reached.

The steps that have been discussed here might be stated in the form of a series of questions, as follows:

1. What is the true problem stated in its present form as I face it?
2. Do I really wish to know the answer to the problem?
3. What is the background of the problem?
4. What are the different aspects or subproblems involved, and how are they interrelated?
5. Where can I find information that will aid in the solution of the problem?
6. What are the various possible answers?
7. Which answer seems most plausible in terms of the supporting evidence?
8. Do I honestly believe the conclusion I have reached?

EXAMPLES OF PROBLEM SOLVING

A teacher may utilize problem situations in all of the various phases of studying a lesson: to launch a new unit of study or a particular subtopic within a unit; to reinforce learning as the study progresses; or to summarize or culminate the unit activity.

When introducing the unit on credit, for example, instead of assigning the lesson to be read, the teacher might pose a problem in the form of a question or a case situation. One such situation would be the student without any lunch money. Another might be the woman who discovers as she approaches the check-out counter that her wallet is missing. Through the ensuing discussion of how these persons might work out their situations, the idea of credit needed by the student or the woman is extended to the use of credit in the business world--by individuals and by businesses. Thus, the three C's of credit are developed by the students themselves as they discuss the problem and proceed later to discover the answers they need. Using this method, they are much more interesting and meaningful to the students than if they are simply memorized as part of the assignment.

Another example of the problem-solving method which is given in the booklet, Let's Educate Youth for Effective Business Life,[2] follows:

Subject

Business-government relationships.

Problem

A local sales tax is about to be increased. Students wish to find out if they are getting their money's worth for their tax dollars.

The teacher and students prepare a checklist designed to reveal what students think about sales taxes and their attitudes toward such taxes. Once these checklists have been completed by the students, the teacher can discover what misconceptions should be corrected and how the students should be guided in studying this problem.

Because tax problems are usually controversial, a panel of students with a student moderator will discuss the question. To prepare for the panel discussion, the class can be divided into committees to gather information. For instance, one committee could visit local tax offices. Another could poll some consumers and businessmen. A third could prepare visual aids, such as

---

[2]The report of a conference sponsored by New York University and financed by a grant from the Esso Standard Oil Company. It was later republished as Monograph 98 by the South-Western Publishing Company.

charts and graphs, to show the relationship of tax increases to
personal income or to the increased cost of local government.
Other students could check the library.

As the culminating activity, the panel members are chosen by
the class, and the discussion is held. At its conclusion all
class members have an opportunity to express their opinions.

Then students respond to the checklist given earlier. Thus,
they see how their ideas and attitudes about taxes have changed.

CASE SITUATIONS

Students respond to a challenge, and the use of case situations is an excellent way to present such challenges. There are
four basic patterns used in case situations.

Pattern One

One way to use case situations is simply to describe the
problem situation and ask students for their solutions. This is
the most common pattern.

Pattern Two

A second procedure is to describe the problem situation and
then to assist the students in their analysis by asking specific
questions. The following two examples are of this type.

Example A

Helen Carson had completed her secretarial course and applied
for a position at the Jasper Company and also at the Rogers Corporation. She was first interviewed by the Rogers Corporation for a

very desirable position at a good beginning salary. The personnel manager at the Rogers Corporation told her that he would let her know by phone if she were to be employed.

While waiting to hear from the Rogers Corporation, Helen was interviewed by the Jasper Company and was offered a position immediately with the understanding that she would report for work in one week. She accepted the offer and agreed to start work the following Monday.

Three days before she was to begin working at the Jasper Company, the personnel manager at the Rogers Corporation called to inform her that she had been selected for the secretarial position with that company. As the salary at the Rogers Corporation was considerably higher than that at the Jasper Company, she was tempted to change her mind and renege on her agreement with the Jasper Company.

1. Does Helen have any obligation to the Rogers Corporation? If so, what is the extent?

2. Does Helen have an obligation to the Jasper Company? If so, what is it? Is it a legal or moral obligation?

3. Does Helen have an obligation to herself? If so, what is it?

4. What would be the best thing for Helen, considering only the present and the immediate future?

5. What would be the best thing for Helen, considering a long period of time? Why?

6. What would you do in a similar situation? Why?

Example B

David, who works in the Payroll Department, is in charge of writing all salary checks and distributing them to the employees. In delivering the checks last month, David made an error and handed the wrong check to Mr. Howard in the Public Relations Department. After opening the envelope, Mr. Howard realized that the check did not belong to him, but belonged to Harry Smith.

Mr. Howard was quite surprised to discover that Harry's salary was considerably more per week than his, as their responsibilities appeared to him to be equal.

    1.   What should Mr. Howard do when he first discovers that an error has been made in delivering the check?

    2.   Do you think Mr. Howard is justified in complaining to his department head about the difference in salary? If your answer is yes, how should he approach the department head?

    3.   Should Mr. Howard say anything to Harry about the difference in their salaries? If so, what should he say? If not, why not?

    4.   Does David have any responsibility here? Is there anything he can do about this situation? If so, what can he do?

Pattern Three

A third pattern is to describe a case situation and then suggest various alternate solutions. The student chooses one of the alternatives and then gives reasons why he made that choice. An example of this pattern follows.

A Personal Services Decision[3]

Jane Wagers, a tenth grader at Madison High School, is a producer because she provides a service by baby-sitting. She is employed regularly on weekends by Mr. and Mrs. Larson and receives $1 an hour with her average monthly income being about $15. She also receives various fringe benefits, such as permission to raid the refrigerator, use the telephone, and use the Larsons' new colored television set. Jane can usually study if she wishes

---

[3]This case situation and the one following are adaptations from two cases included in "Economic Cases for Discussion," developed by Phi Chapter of Delta Pi Epsilon.

to because the baby goes to sleep early. Jane has a steady job with the Larsons.

One evening about two hours before Jane was to baby-sit at the Larsons', Mrs. Quill called and asked for her services. When Jane told her that she already had a job for the evening, Mrs. Quill appealed to her emotions by saying that she just had to have her because some of Mr. Quill's business associates had arrived in town unexpectedly; they had to take them to dinner, and their 18-month-old baby could not be left alone. She continued, "We'd be willing to pay you $6 for the evening, and we'll be back within two and a half hours."

What should Jane do?

1. Jane should accept Mrs. Quill's offer of $6 for the evening.

2. Jane should fulfill her obligation to Mr. and Mrs. Larson.

3. Jane should refer Mrs. Quill to one of her dependable girl friends and fulfill her previous commitment.

4. Jane should tell Mr. and Mrs. Larson that she wants more money because she has been offered more than $1 an hour.

5. Jane should simply tell Mrs. Quill that she is not available that evening.

Explain your choice and give your reasons for selecting it.

Pattern Four

The fourth pattern is similar to that just described except that several possible reasons are stated, as well as alternative solutions. The student chooses the reason from those supplied which is compatible with the solution alternative that he has selected. An example of this type is given here.

An Employer-Employee Wage Decision

Al Rogers has worked for a local department store for two years selling men's furnishings. At the end of six months he received a small increase in wages and another small raise at the end of a year. He received a third modest raise at the end of his second year of employment. Al thought he was doing a good job because his work had never been criticized, and he seemed to be well-liked by his supervisor and fellow workers. He thought that under these circumstances he should have received a larger raise at the end of his second year than the one he received.

What should Al do?

1. Al should not ask for a larger raise because his employer apparently feels that he does not deserve it.

2. Al should go to his employer and explain that he needs more money to meet his obligations.

3. Al should ask his employer what he thinks his opportunities are with the company and what future raises he might expect.

4. Al should take inventory of other employment opportunities for which he is qualified and then decide whether to ask his employer for a raise.

5. Al should make a list of his assets in terms of his contributions to the firm and discuss them with his employer.

Reason(s)

1. Employers should raise their workers' salaries every year.

2. Employers make money on their employees' services and should be willing to give them a large share of it.

3. Well-paid employees produce more than poorly paid employees.

4. Wages are governed by the law of supply and demand.

5. Wages are influenced by the productivity of workers and the efficiency of management.

6. Competition is the controlling factor in wage determination.

7. Employers generally pay their workers what they are worth without being urged to do so.

QUESTIONS, ACTIVITIES, AND PROJECTS

1. Which of the steps in problem solving do you feel is the most important one? Why?

2. Do you prefer wording the steps as indicative statements or as questions? Why?

3. Of the four patterns of case situations described in this chapter, which do you think is the easiest? The hardest?

4. Refer to the case situation about Helen Carson, described earlier in this chapter.

   a. What other questions might have been used?

   b. Would you recommend substituting any of your new questions for any that are used in the chapter?

   c. Would you recommend adding any questions to those used?

5. Refer to the personal services decision that Jane Wagers faced. If you were modifying it to fit pattern four, what list of reasons would you suggest to be used?

6. Refer to the employer-employee wage decision situation described in this chapter.

   a. Choose an alternative course of action, and choose one reason that you feel supports your action choice.

   b. Do you think most high school students would make the same choices? Why or why not?

7. Prepare a case situation following any of the patterns described in this chapter.

8. Select an economic principle which you feel is important that business students understand. List several concepts that relate to that principle. (Examples of principles are: the law of supply and demand, the profit incentive, alternative cost of a product, wants versus scarcity, collective bargaining.)

Evaluation is a means of determining how much students have learned . . . and how well a teacher has taught.

CHAPTER 8

Determining If Learning and Teaching Are Effective

Evaluation in basic business subjects is concerned with estimating and measuring student accomplishment in relation to the objectives of the course. It attempts to ascertain the degree to which both student and teacher goals have been realized. Evaluation is much broader than testing, for it is concerned with observation and research techniques, attitude formation, concept development, and changes in behavior as well as measurement of the acquisition and comprehension of factual information.

The purposes of evaluation are:

1. To provide for the collection of evidence which will show how well students are progressing toward curricular goals.
2. To permit teachers to determine the effectiveness of curricular experiences and instructional methods.
3. To make provisions for guiding the growth of students.
4. To diagnose student strengths and weaknesses.
5. To discover areas where remedial measures are needed.
6. To provide a basis for making changes in the curriculum.

In order to measure accurately the degree to which students have acquired economic competence--the development of which is the chief goal of general business--it would be necessary to observe student performance in life as citizens. However, there are intermediate goals leading to economic competence that can be measured with reasonable accuracy by using a variety of methods. Good evaluation requires the use of both formal and informal instruments, techniques, and processes. It includes observational procedures, rating scales, questionnaires, checklists, conferences, case studies, and self-ratings by students. All information available must be utilized in order to analyze and interpret correctly student progress toward expected outcomes.

Considered in this chapter are: what should be evaluated in basic business classes; techniques and tools used in evaluation; specific suggestions for preparing and using tests; and some principles for assigning school marks.

WHAT SHOULD BE EVALUATED?

In basic business classes teachers are concerned with evaluating the learning and understanding of factual information, student attitudes, performance in research, concept development, and behavior changes.

Knowledge and Understanding of Business Information

The textbook is the basis of class discussion and assignments. It is the one guide and source of information available to and used by all students. It represents an organized body of knowledge about business which the students read from one week to the next. It contains many facts, business terms, and business principles of interest and value to everyone. It provides the basic information about the topics the class discusses.

Teachers and students expand and supplement the textbook material through reading current periodical literature, booklets, and pamphlets available in the classroom, and reference books in the school library.

A number of simple measures can be used to determine whether students have learned business and economic information. Pretests reveal what students know, or do not know, before the study of a topic begins. Short tests given frequently show what is being learned as the class progresses through the textbook. But true vocabulary comprehension depends on understanding how these terms and principles correctly relate to business. Students' achievements in this area may be measured through participation in class discussion and comprehension illustrated in written compositions.

Attitudes Toward Business Principles

An attitude is the way a person feels toward an idea or statement. An individual may be strongly for or against an idea or lukewarm in either direction. But how a person feels (his attitude) exerts great influence in determining how that individual will behave in any given situation. At the one extreme is the person who never questions the motives of others, their truthfulness, or the accuracy of their knowledge. At the other extreme is the individual who trusts no one and is skeptical of all. Between these extremes are varying gradations of each point of view, depending upon the topic involved and the circumstances surrounding the situation. Teachers encourage the development of desirable attitudes on the part of students and attempt to discourage undesirable ones. Attitudes which will enable the students to maximize learning opportunities and assist them in business and social activities should be nurtured by the teacher. Students should be encouraged to develop a positive attitude towards such traits as honesty, punctuality, dependability, courtesy, and friendliness.

Daily observation of students is one means of assisting them in discovering their attitudes. Another means is the attitude inventory. (Since there are no correct or incorrect answers, it is most appropriate to call this instrument an inventory rather than a test.) In basic business courses, such questionnaires can be designed to explore student attitudes toward specific topics. The following is an example of such an instrument designed to explore student attitudes toward the use of credit.

Attitude Inventory Toward Credit

Directions: Indicate your reaction to each of the following statements by stating whether you (1) agree, (2) partially agree, (3) disagree, or (4) are uncertain. For each statement write one of the words: agree, partially, disagree, or uncertain in the appropriate answer space provided.

1. Persons who buy with cash are better financial managers than those who buy on credit. _____

2. Paying cash helps prevent one from buying things he doesn't need. _____

3. The dollar cost to buy on credit is more important than the percentage rate it costs. _____

4. The use of charge accounts encourages a person to overbuy. _____

5. Customers who buy on credit should be charged more than those who pay cash. _____

6. People should not buy on credit, for it discourages the practice of thrift. _____

7. Credit is largely for the rich and should be avoided by poor people. _____

8. The advantages of buying on credit outweigh the disadvantages. _____

9. Borrowing money to pay for an expensive item is better than buying on the instalment plan. _____

10. Buying goods on credit lowers a consumer's standard of living. _____

11. Buying on credit should be limited to the purchase of goods that last a long time. _____

12. Buying goods on credit influences the amount of goods produced in this country. _____

13. A person who buys goods on credit can own more goods than if he always pays cash. _____

Attitudes, which are related to behavior, can probably be measured as accurately by observation as by any other means. A student's reaction to classroom discussions, his particular views and the manner in which he presents them, and whether or not he shows respect for points of view as expressed by others are all indications of his attitude. Items on which opinions are widely divergent provide the basis for interesting class discussions. Teachers who do not encourage such discussion deprive themselves of the opportunity to make needed observations. Furthermore, through discussion misconceptions are clarified, and attitudes may be developed, modified, or improved. Most importantly, the student who seldom questions anything will learn to seek reasons for holding certain opinions about the statements he hears and reads.

Ability to Research Answers to Questions and Problems

Some students learn early in their school life how to do research for information they do not already know. Others must be taught this skill after they enroll in basic business classes. Obviously it represents an ability needed by everyone who is engaged in formal learning experiences or in solving various types of problems.

Since students in basic business courses are taught to use the standard reference books in the area of business, the teacher needs to evaluate their ability to use them. This can be done best by appraising their performance in using them to locate specific types of information. For example, the teacher might ask the students to find the latest statistics on the gross national product, the rate of economic growth, population growth or migration, earnings per capital or per family, or changes in interest rates or credit restrictions. All of these questions are treated in business periodicals, such as Business Week and Forbes, or in current events periodicals, such as Newsweek and the U.S. News & World Report. Students may find these articles by using the Reader's Guide to Periodical Literature. Also fairly recent data of this type may be found in the Economic Almanac, the Statistical Abstract of the United States, or the World Almanac.

Evaluation is concerned with determining if students know where to look and if they can find the exact data desired and do so rapidly and effectively. Evaluation is also concerned with the students' ability to interpret data correctly and apply it to assignments. The teacher accomplishes this by observing the students as they use reference materials in the library or classroom and by determining the recentness and appropriateness of the data they obtain.

Ability to Develop Insights and Reasoning

The evaluation of students' comprehension of ideas and their interrelationships is more important and more difficult than testing their mastery of simple factual information. Instruments designed to measure insights must provide answers that give reasons supporting the positions they hold.

In the solution of problems one must consider all alternate courses of action that are feasible. So the evaluation of the students' understanding of principles is accomplished through the use of case situations with accompanying alternate solutions. Students are asked to choose the most logical solution and then choose a reason that supports the solution they select.

Teachers should prepare brief cases with alternate solutions dealing with the specific topic currently being studied. The students draw upon their general knowledge and understanding of the topic and the specific facts or principles involved in the problem situation described. When studying the marketing process, for example, students learn that wholesalers, retailers, and transportation companies render certain types of services between the time that an article is produced and the time that it is de-

livered to its ultimate consumer. In some cases the wholesaler
or retailer may be by-passed, but the services he normally renders must be performed just the same--in this case by one of the
other parties involved in the distribution process. One process
by which teachers may check to see if the students understand
this principle is illustrated here.

An Example

The Principle	The functions of marketing may be performed by different agencies in the distribution process, but they cannot be eliminated.
The Situation	Mr. Bellomy has observed that the retail price of eggs in the local grocery stores is approximately twice the amount he receives for eggs he delivers to the wholesale produce house. In order to receive a higher price for his eggs he is considering selling them directly to the consumers. He will purchase a pickup truck and employ a driver to deliver the eggs in cardboard cartons to customers' houses.
Answer Choices	1. Mr. Bellomy's plan is sound. He can make more money than he has been making because he will receive more for his eggs.
	2. His plan is not a wise one. He will make less money than formerly.
	3. His plan will not work, for he cannot carry it out.
	4. His plan may work, but he will not make much more profit than he now makes--maybe not as much.
Reasons for the Choice	1. If Mr. Bellomy wants the job done right, he should do it himself.
	2. There will be problems, but a man of Mr. Bellomy's ability can meet them.
	3. The cost of putting eggs in cartons and delivering them is about the same regardless of who performs the service.

4. The cost of processing and delivering the eggs would exceed the extra income he would receive because of his small number of customers.

5. Middlemen charge too much for the services they render because they do not increase the value of the products they handle.

A student who selects "answer number 2" should choose "reason number 4" to justify his selection. One who selects "answer number 4" should choose "reason number 3" to justify his selection. Either of these pairs of choices would indicate that the student understands the marketing function that has been studied and that he can reason from the knowledge he has attained.

A modification of this measuring instrument is to use the same situation but give only one plausible solution. The student indicates whether or not he agrees with the solution offered and the degree to which he agrees or disagrees and writes in his own words the reasons for his decision.

Changes in Behavior

Changes in student behavior may be evaluated through the use of rating scales. An individual student rates himself on some particular type of activity, such as participation as a committee member. As a check against his ratings the teacher (or another student) also rates him. The ratings thus obtained on any given day will be an index of his conduct at that time. By comparing these ratings with those that were attained at an earlier date, the degree of improvement during the interval is shown. An example of such a rating scale follows.

Rating Scale

Measuring Individual Participation in Committee Work

	Activity	Value	Description	Score
1.	Offering suggestions	5	Volunteers worthwhile suggestions	
		3	Occasionally gives good suggestions	
		2	Offers suggestions when requested	
		1	Makes some contributions	_____
2.	Listening	5	Seems intently interested in the contributions of others	
		3	Listens when others talk but with little apparent interest	
		2	Does not interrupt others' conversations	
		1	Tolerates others' contributions but does not appreciate them	_____
3.	Accepting share of work	5	Volunteers to do more than is expected of him	
		3	Volunteers to do his fair share	
		2	Does his share when it is assigned	
		1	Accepts responsibility for minor tasks only	_____
4.	Accepting group decisions	5	Willingly accepts and carries out decisions of the majority	
		3	Accepts group decisions but not enthusiastically	
		2	Agrees to majority decisions but does not work to carry them out	
		1	Accepts group decisions reluctantly	_____

TECHNIQUES AND TOOLS USED IN EVALUATION

Fortunately teachers have available to them a variety of means for use in evaluation. The use of inventories and rating scales has already been illustrated. In addition to these, teachers may use student participation during class discussions, written assignments, special reports (both oral and written), project books, and displays. Written examinations will be covered separately. Each of these is sufficiently important to warrant special attention.

Class Participation

In every class there are students who consistently study their textbooks, prepare their assignments, and recite in class. In evaluating individual students on class discussion, the quality as well as the frequency of their participation should be considered. There are different levels of student participation in class recitation. Occasionally one class member will attempt to monopolize class discussion. Though he talks often he seldom actually says much. Others may contribute only occasionally, but what they say is usually acceptable, though it may not be outstanding. Some students can discuss intelligently the specific material assigned but never go beyond what they have memorized from the book. The ideal students supplement the text material by regularly contributing items of current interest reported in the newspapers and magazines.

Some students may contribute regularly and well but never get beyond the level of reporting. They can recite about the material in the book and tell about what they have seen or read. But when it comes to interpreting, appraising a point of view, or applying it to new situations, they fall far short. Other students may not research out supplementary current information, but

they are able to evaluate opinions well. They can reason logically and analyze problem situations correctly.

It goes without saying that the teacher has an obligation to
teach students how to participate in class activities and how to
improve their abilities to participate on progressively higher
levels, as well as to evaluate their performance. Students can
be helped to evaluate themselves on the quality of their class
contributions through the use of a checklist or inventory. An
example of such an inventory follows.

Inventory of Class Participation

Directions: After each statement, write the word that best describes your practices: seldom, sometimes, or
usually.

1. I try to stay alert at all times during class
discussion.   _____

2. When the teacher questions my classmates, I
listen to the students' answers and try to
answer the questions for myself.   _____

3. I make notes of items the teacher emphasizes
and/or writes on the board.   _____

4. I ask specific questions on matters I do not
understand.   _____

5. I write down my assignments carefully at the
time they are made.   _____

6. I try to make a contribution of some kind each
day.   _____

7. I try not to monopolize the time in class.   _____

8. When I give an incorrect reply in class, I try
to understand why I am wrong and correct my
mistake.   _____

9. I try to supplement the textbook from library
resources.   _____

10. As I study, I choose specific items to recite
on during the next class period.   _____

11. I study the case problems, try to solve them,
and offer my opinions regarding their solutions.   _____

12. I volunteer for extra work or special reports
that require out-of-class preparation.   _____

13. I take the responsibility for making up work
I have missed.   _____

Written Assignments

Most teachers of basic business subjects use a variety of written assignments--answers to problems and questions which normally appear at the end of textbook chapters, materials found in the study guide and workbook, and a wide assortment of special assignments--to evaluate student progress. The completion of this work is accepted as evidence that the student has spent some time in lesson preparation. The degree of completeness and correctness of a student's answers constitutes the quality of this written work. In many instances a grade or mark is placed on his homework, while in others the student is simply given credit for having done the work. Usually a record of some type is kept in the teacher's class record book.

Oral and Written Reports

Most students will volunteer for some type of special study requiring out-of-class reading and research. The student will then report orally to the entire class. His report will be incorporated into a committee's report, or it will become a written report to the teacher--in some cases a term paper.

These reports are generally considered to be satisfactory instruments for evaluating the quality of an individual's research. His ability to choose worthwhile items from those he has investigated, to organize ideas in an orderly manner, and to express his ideas correctly, logically, and interestingly is the criterion used in evaluating this work.

Both oral and written reports can be effective evaluative instruments because they cover several facets of student achievement, and they may be used satisfactorily by students of widely varying interests and abilities.

Project Books and Displays

Project Books. Project books are an excellent evaluative tool because of their flexibility and versatility. They may be brief or comprehensive; there is hardly any limit to what students can do with them. They may include a wide variety of items in their project books, such as class notes, notes on outside readings, newspaper or periodical clippings, pictures, cartoons, sketchings or drawings, charts, graphs, and diagrams.

Teachers may use the following criteria to evaluate students' project books: the extent of the material; the appropriateness of the content; the neatness and appearance of the book; and the nature and thoroughness of the organization. Grades on project books will usually vary widely because of the differences in the skills, interests, and abilities of the class members. Probably no other activity affords more opportunities for students to exercise initiative and demonstrate their interest in a topic than do project books.

Displays. The use of bulletin-board exhibits, and the collections of items, such as pamphlets, canceled checks, realia, etc., has been discussed previously. Like project books, they are an excellent evaluation instrument because they allow students to exercise their individual skills. They are good indicators of student interest and ability and should be evaluated according to quality, thoroughness, originality, and extensiveness.

WRITTEN EXAMINATIONS AS EVALUATION INSTRUMENTS

The topic of examinations as evaluation instruments is sufficiently extensive to justify devoting considerable space to its discussion. An examination, or test, is undoubtedly the evaluation instrument most used by business teachers. When properly prepared and administered, it constitutes an excellent measure of student achievement. Regardless of the type of examination employed, the following general principles should be observed:

1. It should measure mastery of the items considered to be important.

2. It should be written in a clear and concise manner, free of ambiguity.

3. It should employ a vocabulary consistent with the ability level of those being tested.

4. The information in one part of the test should not supply the answers for items in another section. (Reading the entire test through after he has completed it, the student may discover this error and use the information to change or complete his answers, reducing the validity of the test as an evaluation tool.)

5. The active interest of the student should be maintained throughout the examination. This may be accomplished by progressing from the easiest items at the beginning of the test to the hardest at the end and by having a variety of forms of items.

Using Subjective Examinations

Subjective examinations put test items in problem or essay form and draw upon the knowledge of the students to solve the problems or answer the questions.

They require students to organize their thoughts, choose words to express their ideas, and frame their replies in sentences that make clear the meaning they have in mind. This makes it essential that the teacher word a question so that its meaning and intent are clear to the students.

Teachers can help students know how to answer a question if they explain to them beforehand the differences in the meanings of clue words so often employed in subjective test items. For example, to explain, to outline, to compare, to summarize, or to illustrate all have different meanings. One of the best ways to accomplish this is through the use of definitions and examples.

A summary list of these, when supplied to students and discussed with them, will prove most helpful. The following are examples.

Types of Subjective Test Items

1. COMPARE--Show similarities or resemblances; unlikenesses and dissimilarities.

    (Example)

    Compare the information that is written on a check with that on the check stub. (What items are included on both? What items on the check only? What items on the stub only?)

2. CRITICIZE--Point out errors or weaknesses or find fault with the items; criticize may mean to point out the strong or good point of an item.

    (Example)

    Criticize briefly the statement: Insurance companies should offer no more than two types of policies to the public.

3. DEFINE--Give a short, clear, and accurate statement; do not discuss in detail; do not give illustrations unless requested.

    (Example)

    Define "dividends" as used in connection with insurance policies.

4. EXPLAIN--Give a clear picture by telling and showing; an illustration may help.

    (Example)

    Explain how a person can tell the difference between a counterfeit bill and a genuine bill.

5. ILLUSTRATE--Give a good, clear, and pertinent example, instance, or case; omit definitions.

    (Example)

    Illustrate how you would endorse a check restricting its transfer to some specific purpose.

6. LIST OR NAME--Write only a simple series of items; do not discuss or illustrate.

    (Example)

       <u>List</u> the five elements necessary to make a contract valid.

7. OUTLINE--Give the main point only; no details; little or no discussion; show relationships.

    (Example)

       <u>Outline</u> the advantages of savings accounts which make them highly desirable for high school students.

8. PROVE OR JUSTIFY--List the arguments in favor of the statement; a list of arguments against the statement may also be helpful.

    (Example)

       <u>Read</u> the following contract and <u>prove</u> whether or not the contract is fraudulent: A solicitor for the school newspaper tells a prospective advertiser, "If you purchase this space, all of the students in school will buy from you."

9. STATE--Express ideas briefly and clearly; do not discuss in detail or illustrate.

    (Example)

       <u>Give</u> examples of claims that may be held against real estate with which a prospective buyer should be familiar.

10. SUMMARIZE--In a short and concise manner sum up the main points; do not discuss or explain in detail; do not illustrate.

    (Example)

       <u>Summarize</u> the essential principles to be observed when a person makes a will.

11. EXPLAIN WHY--Give causes, reasons, or effects.

    (Example)

       <u>Explain</u> why the check stub should be completed before a person writes a check.

Essay type questions from simplest to most complex are: (1) what, who, when, which, where; (2) list; (3) outline; (4) describe; (5) explain; (6) compare; (7) contrast; (8) discuss; (9) develop; (10) summarize; and (11) evaluate.

Procedures for Answering Subjective Questions

Teachers can expect quality performances from students only after they have had instruction and practice in correct procedures for answering subjective questions. Such instruction should include the following suggestions:

Plan Before Starting to Write

1. Read the directions carefully and follow them closely; underscore clue words and descriptive terms.
2. Make a survey of all questions first.
3. If you are allowed options, make your selections.
4. In selecting options, choose those which are related.
5. If you are allowed to select questions, be certain that you answer only the number indicated.
6. In general, answer the easiest and shortest questions first.
7. Plan a time schedule for your examination.
8. Be sure you understand a question before beginning to write your answer.
9. Do all that is asked, but no more. Remember that the ability to understand and follow directions is one of the marks of intelligence.

As You Write

1. Organize your thoughts and outline your answer before attempting to put it on paper.
2. Answer the question fully but do not overanswer it.
3. Stick to the question; do not include statements that are not pertinent to it.
4. If you are unable to give a complete answer, write what you can.
5. Do not try to bluff--it's ideas, not words, that count.

6. If you change your mind and write another answer to a question, be sure to indicate which answer you wish to have read.

7. Leave some space at the end of each answer so that if you wish to make additional comments later you may do so.

8. Give your answers a final reading if time permits.

Preparing Subjective Test Items

There are a number of guidelines that help teachers prepare high-quality subjective questions. Each question should be planned to measure a single objective of instruction. Before starting to word a question, one should have clearly in mind the thought processes that the question is intended to bring out. Such phrases as "what do you think," "in your opinion," or "write all you know about," should be avoided. Questions should be written in such a way as to require a definite answer.

Objectivity may be brought into the evaluation of answers of essay questions by structuring the organizational pattern desired in the answer. By "fencing in" the question, an item is made definite enough that the students know what is expected of them. This is done by asking for a specific type of discussion, rather than permitting a completely free-wheeling type of reply. Rather than simply asking students to discuss a certain topic, the question might ask students to explain the provisions of, the circumstances surrounding, or the reasons why. Or students might be asked to describe the attempts that were made, the important qualities of, or the distinguishing features of. Other instructions might be to prepare a chart, make comparisons, or give examples.

Here are some essay-type questions based on the topic of insurance.

1. Explain the basic principle under which insurance operates.

2. Describe the factors that must be considered when choosing an insurance agent.

3. <u>Name</u> the <u>various kinds</u> of automobile insurance protection available and <u>indicate what types</u> of coverage each kind <u>includes</u>.

4. <u>Who pays</u> for social security, <u>who benefits</u> from it, and <u>what types of benefits</u> does it provide?

5. <u>Prepare a chart</u> showing a comparison of the special features of the <u>four principal types</u> of life insurance policies.

The longer and more involved a question is, the more difficult it is to answer satisfactorily. Some students will not understand what is to be done. Others will complete one element but overlook others. An example of such a question follows:

1. Name the four principal kinds of life insurance coverage, give the chief characteristics of each, and describe a situation for each type wherein it would be particularly suitable.

There are three different things to be done here: <u>name kinds</u>, <u>give characteristics</u>, and <u>describe situations</u>. It would be much better to break this question into parts as follows:

1. Name and describe the special features of the four principal kinds of life insurance policies.

2. Describe problem situations in which persons might buy a particular type of life insurance coverage. Describe a situation for each of the four main types of policies.

Marking Subjective Questions

There are a few simple procedures that improve the quality of evaluation when grading essay questions. In the first place, the teacher should have in mind what would constitute an ideal or complete answer. One way to accomplish this is to outline a standard answer to the question before reading the students' answers. Naturally, the teacher would not expect many students to do as well as he, although in some instances they may even exceed the teacher's solution. But the teacher's outline of the main points included in a particular question will provide a standard to which the students' answers may be compared.

A second helpful procedure is to read all answers to a particular question before going on to the next question. This will give uniformity in the number of points awarded for similar partially acceptable answers. If the teacher marks all the answers on one student's paper before examining another student's paper, he will not remember how much credit he gave for an answer to a particular question which he read earlier and which was of the same caliber.

It is also helpful if a teacher will read the answers to a certain question from three or four papers before deciding upon a point value for any of them. This gives the teacher an idea of how well the question was handled generally.

It is important to have students write their names on the back of the last page of their examination paper only and then staple all sheets together. In this way the teacher does not know whose paper is being read and, therefore, does not have his opinions biased because of knowing that the writer is a "good" or "poor" student. It is also important that a teacher not permit his evaluation of student answers to be influenced by irrelevant factors, such as poor penmanship or lack of neatness.

Using Objective Examinations

The objective type of examination eliminates the judgment factor in scoring. Each question has a definite answer and papers are scored by using a key which is prepared beforehand. The most commonly used types of objective items are true-false, completion, matching, and multiple-choice. The first three forms are largely recall types. Multiple-choice items employ both recall and decision making.

Preparing Objective Test Items

When preparing objective tests, one should begin with approximately twice as many items as he will eventually use. The easiest items should appear first in the examinations, progressing to the most difficult items, which are placed last. The range of difficulty should be such that no student makes a zero or a perfect score. Items should be worded positively rather than negatively, and words such as <u>always</u>, <u>never</u>, <u>only</u>, <u>seldom</u>, and <u>often</u> should be avoided.

Simple, clear directions should be given, and sample questions should be provided. Each item should contain only one idea or factor. Each item should stand alone, that is, not be dependent upon any other item.

There are a few principles that apply to the specific types of objective items. The most important of these are given here.

True-False Items

1. Use relatively short and simple sentences, each approximately the same length.

2. Avoid using either too many true items or too many false items. Approximately half the items should be true and half false.

3. Avoid items that are partly true and partly false.

4. Use items that cannot be answered easily by a good guess.

5. Eliminate the factor of guessing. Have the students explain why an item is false or correct it to make it true.

Sample Items

Directions: Each of the following statements is either true or false. If the statement is true, write the word "<u>true</u>" at the right; if it is false, write the word "<u>false</u>."

1. The most important purpose of budgeting is to learn how to prepare financial reports.   1._____

2. Estimating one's income for a future period is a good starting point in preparing a budget.   2._____

3. A record of past expenditures is a good guide for planning future spending.   3._____

Completion Items

1. Put the blanks in the statement near the end of the sentence and use only one blank in each statement.

2. Do not give a clue by using "a" or "an" but show both--a (an).

3. Provide only one unbroken line, even though two words may be needed to complete a statement.

4. Make all answer lines the same length.

5. Make sure the statement is clear, even with the answer part omitted.

6. Do not use sentences exactly as they are worded in the text.

Sample Items

Directions: Each of the following sentences can be completed correctly by supplying the appropriate word or words. Write these words on the lines provided for them.

1. A bank's record of the way a customer signs his name is the _____.   1._____

2. The person to whom a check is made payable is known as the _____.   2._____

3. The form on which items to be credited in one's bank account are listed is a (an) _____.   3._____

Matching Items

1. Make the answer list several items longer than the question list.

2. Arrange the answer list in alphabetical order.

3. Place the answer list on the same page as the question list.

4. Indicate in the directions that an answer may be used more than once, if this be true.

Sample Items

Directions: For each of the following statements, some term in the column at the left matches it in meaning. Write the letter that precedes this term in the answer space provided.

a. bank
b. collateral
c. credit union
d. maker
e. payee
f. principal

1. A cooperative loan agency that lends money to its members only   1._____

2. Property that is pledged as security for a loan   2._____

3. The person who signs a promissory note   3._____

4. The amount of a loan   4._____

Multiple-Choice Items

1. Give the same number of choices for each item--four choices are preferable to three or five.

2. Give choices which are all plausible, but only one which is correct. One choice should contain specific information, or qualifying information, that makes it the correct answer. All other choices should be sufficiently plausible that students who do not know the correct answer might choose them.

3. Make the main stem complete in meaning so that it stands alone--one should not have to read the answer choices in order to grasp the meaning of the item.

4. Make all answer choices approximately equal in length.

5. Construct all answer choices so that they are grammatically similar.

6. Arrange answer choices in some systematic order or sequence. (Numbers should appear in sequence; and names, in alphabetical order.)

7. Word items positively. When the best order requires the choice that does NOT conform to the statement given in the stem, the word not should be underscored.

8. Avoid the overuse of "all of the above/none of the above." Do not use both in the same item.

Directions: Each of the following statements can be completed correctly with one of the items listed. Choose this item and write the letter that precedes your choice on the line provided at the right.

1. The process of getting goods from producer to consumer is (a) assembling, (b) distribution, (c) manufacturing, (d) processing.   1._____

2. Putting goods away temporarily in a safe place is (a) aging, (b) assembling, (c) collecting, (d) storing.   2._____

3. Goods that are likely to spoil soon are (a) durable, (b) packaged, (c) perishable, (d) stable.   3._____

Designing the Test Format

The format in which a test is designed can be important to the teacher as well as to the students. A uniformly prepared test will save the students time in answering the test questions, and it will do the same for the teacher who grades the examination.

When all blanks are placed in a column at the right edge of the paper, the teacher can prepare a key which can be placed next to the answers, thus making grading a relatively easy task.

Blanks in which the students are to place their answers should be located near the question and should be numbered to coincide with the question to prevent the student from placing answers on the "wrong" line. This numbering process will also enable the teacher to keep the key in proper alignment while grading.

As it is difficult to rewrite basic business test questions year after year, a separate answer sheet might be developed. Thus, the teacher may retain the test sheets but permit the students to have a record of their scores. To prevent subsequent students from memorizing answer patterns from the answer sheets, the teacher need only rearrange the test questions from year to year.

Test Analysis

Once the tests have been graded, the teacher should examine the corrected papers as a means of evaluating the test and the teaching/learning process that took place prior to the examination.

This analysis is done by simply taking an extra copy of the test or key, then making a mark beside the item number each time that question has been missed by a student. These marks are then totaled so that the teacher can determine how many and what percentage of the students missed each question on the test.

If the analysis reveals that a question has been missed by nearly all of the class, that question should not be considered in computing the test scores. It is obvious that the wording of the question was poor or that the teacher or the teaching materials did not sufficiently teach the concept being examined.

If a question has been missed by all but a few students, the papers of those students should be examined individually. If the grades on those students' tests were among the highest, then it may be assumed that the question missed was a discerning one. If, however, the grades on the few students' papers were among the lowest, it is likely that these students chose the correct answer by chance alone. The question, then, is not a discerning one and should be discarded or at least reworded before use on future tests.

If a significant number of students miss questions concerning material the teacher feels is essential to their ability to function as wise consumers or is necessary for the understanding of concepts to be studied later, that material should be retaught.

BASES FOR ASSIGNING SCHOOL MARKS

Almost every school requires teachers to assign marks for report cards and the school's permanent records. Perhaps the most common error committed by basic business teachers when assigning school marks is too heavy a reliance on scores made on written examinations. This is one criterion, of course. However, since in basic business classes students participate in a wide variety of activities--committee work, special reports, projects--their performance in connection with all their activities should be taken into consideration.

One general business teacher uses the following form in evaluating his students. The percentages after each type of performance are those used in determining the students' unit grades.

General Business--Unit O

Evaluation of _____
(Name of Student)

1. Unit test   20%   Grade _____
2. Weekly quizzes   20%   Grade _____
3. Oral or written report   20%   Grade _____
4. Class contributions   20%   Grade _____
5. Committee work or
   special projects   20%   Grade _____

                                      Unit Grade _____

A student's semester grade is determined by averaging his unit grades and the grade made on his semester examination. Other teachers use different factors as their bases for evaluation. The preceding form serves only to illustrate how various factors may be taken into consideration in determining grades and is not intended to be followed verbatim. In some cases there may be only four factors or there may be more than five. The list of factors may change, too, from one grading period to another.

QUESTIONS, ACTIVITIES, AND PROJECTS

1. What techniques besides tests may be used for measuring students' knowledge?

2. How may a teacher assess student attitudes?

3. Why is it important to have students evaluate themselves on behavior changes?

4. Why is it advisable to have someone in addition to the student appraise his behavior?

5. What factors would you use in evaluating a term paper or other major written report?

6. For what purposes would subjective examinations be preferred to objective tests?

7. What guides are of the greatest value to students when writing subjective examinations?

8. For each type of objective test item, which single rule or principle do you feel is the most important? Why?

9. Explain several procedures recommended for use when grading subjective examinations.

10. Select one of the following topics and secure recent statistical data pertaining to it, using current periodical literature or the current year's issue of some economic almanac.

> Age distribution of the labor force
> Cost of living
> Economic growth
> Employment and unemployment
> Federal government budget
> Gross national product
> Imports and exports
> Inflation
> Interest rates and money supply
> Personal income
> Population trends
> Shift in family income
> Taxes

11. Prepare a rating scale similar to the one shown earlier in this chapter for these items:

Quality of completed work
Preparing assignments
Sharing knowledge with others
Tolerance of others
Planning during study periods

12. Select one of the following topics normally taught in general business and prepare five subjective examination questions covering that unit:

American business system
Budgeting and buying
Careers in business
The financing of government
Labor and American business

13. Select some topic normally taught in business law or economics. Prepare five true-false, five completion, five matching, and five multiple-choice test items covering that topic. Write directions and give an example for each type of item.

I know my subject matter.
The textbook is excellent.
Why aren't my students learning?

CHAPTER 9

Teaching Methods

The teacher must use a wide variety of teaching methods, for variety is as important in method as it is in learning. Some of the factors that enter into the selection of a specific teaching method for a particular lesson are the needs of the students, the nature of the topic being studied, the type of method employed previously, and the past experience of the class members. This is not intended to be a comprehensive discussion of all general teaching methods, but several have been chosen for discussion here:

1. Class discussion.
2. Questioning.
3. Role playing.
4. Interviews.
5. Field trips.
6. Newspapers and news magazines.
7. Committee work.
8. Study guides.
9. Panels and debates.
10. Oral and written reports.

CLASS DISCUSSION

The very nature of the basic business subjects calls for socialization among students, and class discussion provides a natural give-and-take in a social situation. It may be employed before students have read about the topic at hand or after it has been assigned and studied. The topics and ideas to be discussed may be supplied by the students, by the teacher, or by both.

Decision making is perhaps the highest level of discussion and gives both the individuals and the group experience in reaching conclusions. Factual evidence should be sought as well as opinions. The teacher should be careful to see that some type of summary or interpretation is a part of class discussion. Some examples of realistic discussion items for appropriate basic business classes are now given.

The Business System

1. Explain how the percentage distribution of the population in age-group classifications affects the demand for consumer products.

2. Justify the high cost of distribution in relation to the manufacturing cost--approximately one-half the cost of the product. (Hint: Consider the various types of businesses that share in the distribution and marketing of a finished product.)

Money and Banking

1. Name and discuss various business activities you have had this week that you could not have experienced if no established monetary system existed.

2. Explain several ways that you may purchase goods without the use of money, that is, by using substitutes for money, such as checks or notes.

Government and Business

1. Name and describe the different types of taxes commonly used by state and local governments.

2. Contrast the services that the federal and the state governments render the businesses that operate in your community.

Generating Student Discussion

Active student discussion doesn't "just happen." Discussion must be generated and maintained to be effective, and it is the teacher's role to see that this is done. A good teacher can encourage discussion by adhering to the following basic principles:

1. The teacher should introduce topics which are within the range of students' interests, knowledge, and experience. He should avoid topics which may cause embarrassment to an individual student.

2. The teacher should state the topic to be discussed in a manner that is not ambiguous and cannot be dismissed with a simple response. The topic should not be introduced in a way which implies that there is only one correct response.

3. The teacher should provide an informal, relaxed environment. This may mean rearranging the seats in a circle or in some other informal manner. Discussion may also be enhanced if the teacher remains in a sitting position during student comments.

4. The teacher should encourage students to participate by listening attentively to their responses and by responding positively to their contributions. The teacher should never ridicule student responses or appear intolerant of student contributions.

5. The teacher should not allow one or two students to monopolize the discussion.

6. The teacher should participate in the discussion as little as possible, simply providing guidance and generating further discussion.

7. The teacher should avoid topics which are so controversial that students hesitate to oppose one another for fear of peer disapproval.

The teacher's lesson plans should include all points which he hopes students will include in their discussions. This enables the teacher to generate further discussion and also serves as a backup lecture plan in the event that students are reluctant to engage in class discussion.

QUESTIONING

Questioning lies at the heart of all good social business teaching. So it is important to consider some suggestions aimed at improving the ways that teachers use questions.

Is it possible to begin a lesson presentation with a question that is so pointed that it will instantly stimulate student attention and interest? Should a teacher's very first question point toward the goal he wishes to achieve by the end of the lesson? Are students more interested in their opinions and questions than in the teacher's? Is it true that little teaching or learning takes place until the students begin to ask questions? Should the teacher's questions provoke thought and questions by the students? Should the teacher's questions which are prepared in advance be fraught with purposeful meaning? Should the teacher really know more about the art of making good questions?

Using Questions

Questions may be used for a variety of purposes and they should all be related to the aims of the lesson. Questions may be used to:

1. Introduce a lesson or topic.

   Examples:
   a. If you had been cheated when you purchased an article yesterday, to whom might you report the incident?

   b. If you had money to put in savings, to which of the local savings institutions would you entrust it?

2. Attract attention or hold interest.

   Examples:

   a. If you were injured in an automobile accident and hospitalized, who would pay the bills?

   b. If you needed a few dollars to buy some Christmas presents, by what method would you accumulate the money you need?

3. Stimulate thought.

   Examples:

   a. Why must a country have an established monetary system?

   b. Why does the local government have specific zones for business and others for homes and apartments?

4. Test knowledge.

   Examples:

   a. If you have agreed to sell your car to another person for a given price, must this agreement be in writing for it to be enforceable?

   b. What are the most important factors to consider when borrowing money?

5. Set up a problem situation.

   Examples:

   a. If you reached the cashier in the lunchroom before you discovered you had no money, how could you still eat lunch and satisfy him about paying for it later?

   b. If you were asked to vote for the establishment of a labor union in the place where you work, what factors would you consider in reaching a decision on this matter?

6. Close a discussion.

   Examples:

   a. What part of our discussion still bothers you?

b. What has been the most important thing we have
    learned today?

Handling Student Responses and Questions

The teacher should accept all student responses offered,
being careful not to reject those that are incorrect. If a
teacher rejects a student's responses continually, he may stop
trying to answer questions. But if incorrect answers are offered,
they should be corrected through later discussion.

Students sometimes ask questions that require special handling by the teacher. Some questions may not pertain to the topic
being studied, or, occasionally, the teacher may not know the
answer to a student's question. In both instances the teacher
needs to exercise judgment in deciding how to dispose of the question. It may be better in some instances to answer the question
but in others it may be better to postpone answering it.

When a student's question does not pertain to the topic under consideration it is important that the teacher guard against
being drawn off the subject. A question such as this may be
handled in one of these ways:

1. If it can be answered easily and quickly, the teacher
    should do so and return to the topic at hand.

2. The teacher should acknowledge the question but if it
    relates to a topic to be discussed in the future post-
    pone answering it until the class comes to that topic.

3. The teacher should acknowledge the question and offer to
    answer it for the individual student during the super-
    vised study period.

4. If the question is at all germane to the day's work, the
    teacher should depart momentarily to pursue it but re-
    turn shortly to the main topic being discussed.

When the teacher does not know the answer to a student's
question, he may handle it in any of these ways:

1. The teacher may ask the other class members if any of
    them can answer it.

2. The teacher may ask the student who put forth the question to look it up for tomorrow, then make sure he knows the answer by the next day.

3. The teacher may admit he does not know the exact answer but state that he will find the answer by the next day.

ROLE PLAYING

Role playing (or the sociodrama, as it is sometimes called) is acting out in front of the class situations that illustrate factual information, opinions, ideas, or principles. It represents an attempt to place oneself in the position of others in order to feel or think as they do.

Role playing may be formal or informal, spontaneous or pre-planned. Usually it takes place in a "setting" at the front of the room, but in some instances it may be done by students who occupy their normal stations in the class. When dramatic skits are employed to cover important factual data of considerable scope, or a major principle basic to rationalization or decision making, a script should be prepared. The script might be prepared by the teacher or written by the students.

Should the skit be planned for the purpose of emphasizing essential provisions of the "truth-in-lending law," for example, the use of a script would be the only way to assure that certain salient stipulations of the law were covered.

The advantages of role playing are:

1. It enables students to project themselves into the "shoes" of someone else.

2. It encourages individuals to be uninhibited with others.

3. It affords opportunities for self-expression and builds self-confidence and poise.

4. It gives variety and spice to class study.

5. It encourages students to think and to react to the ideas of others.

6. It encourages students to use imagination and creativity.

155

7. It provides a setting whereby controversial issues may be considered.

Some examples of role-playing possibilities are:

1. Entering into a contract with a door-to-door salesman.
2. Visiting various savings institutions to determine conditions regarding depositing and withdrawing savings.
3. Interviewing for a job.
4. Breaking a contract entered into by a minor and an adult.
5. Taking action in a bailment situation where a neighbor took care (ineffectively) of one's dog.
6. Settling an insurance claim where the accident victim was seriously injured.

Here is the script for a role-playing situation that has been found to be effective in consumer economics. The topic is the inspection and grading of meat as required by the Federal Meat Inspection Act.[1,2]

PURPLE INK

A skit, based on Federal Meat Inspection legislation,
for use in Consumer Education
Approximate running time: 7 minutes

by Ross E. Lowe

Cast of Characters

Larry Thomas: Supermarket Clerk
Roger and Sally Wilson: a Young Married Couple
Mr. Warren: Manager, Supermarket Meat Department

Scene: the Village Supermarket

---

[1]Published in The Journal of Business Education for November, 1969; copyright by Robert C. Treathaway.

[2]For additional role-playing situations, see Monographs 124 and 131, General Business Skits, published by South-Western Publishing Company.

It is late afternoon as Sally and Roger Wilson, a young married couple, approach the meat counter at the Village Supermarket. Larry Thomas is arranging a display and looks up as Sally speaks.

SALLY (handing package to Larry): Will you trim the purple ink off this steak, Larry? I don't see why you can't be more careful and remove impurities before you place the meat on display.

Larry: Certainly, I'll be glad to. Actually, you could cook this beef as it is without any danger to your family. The purple ink marking is a harmless dye used to indicate to you that the meat was inspected and passed by the U.S. Department of Agriculture.

ROGER: Why would that be necessary? Isn't all meat inspected by the Federal Government?

LARRY: Most of it is, but there is no requirement that meat which does not cross State lines be federally inspected.

ROGER: That's news to me! I've been reading all my life about the Meat Inspection Act--and just lately there has been a lot in the paper about the Wholesome Meat Act.

SALLY: Now, Roger, don't be difficult. I'm sure they do the best they can. What I want to know is whether this steak is the very best available. It is "good" grade, isn't it?

LARRY: It is better than good; it's choice. That's the grade our customers prefer and what we carry as a general rule. The highest grade, prime, usually isn't handled by local stores, most of it going to caterers and hotel dining rooms. Good is the third highest grade of beef.

ROGER: Back to the point I was making, Larry. What is the "Wholesome Meat Act"?

LARRY: It is an amendment to the Federal Meat Inspection Act. This more recent Act is an attempt to bring about State meat inspection programs which are at least equal to the Federal inspection program.

ROGER: How does it do this?

LARRY: The Act provides for Federal technical assistance, advice, and even money, for States with cooperating programs. And there is a provision to the effect that if a State does not develop a comparable program within two years from the effective date, Federal inspection requirements may be imposed in that State.

SALLY: When do they inspect animals that are to be used for food?

LARRY: Before slaughter AND after slaughter. And the premises are inspected, too.

ROGER: What do the inspectors look for during the inspection?

LARRY: They are trying to prevent the shipment and sale of adulterated meat and meat products.

SALLY: What does "adulterated" mean?

(Mr. Warren enters, works with display.)

LARRY: I'm afraid I am getting in over my head. Here is Mr. Warren, the manager. Mr. Warren, can you answer some questions about the Federal Meat Inspection Act? They want to know what "adulterated" means.

MR. WARREN: Of course, Larry. Glad to see you, Mr. and Mrs. Wilson. The Act covers over 20 pages of fine print, and I don't know ALL the provisions, but I DO know what they mean by adulterated. For example meat is considered adulterated (writes on meat wrapping paper as he thinks aloud):

One. If it contains any poisonous, decomposed, or other substance which may make it harmful or unfit for human food.

SALLY: I would hope so!

MR. WARREN (continues): Two. If it contains certain pesticides, food or color additives, which under various federal laws are considered unsafe.

ROGER: That's a good thing, too. The average person can't tell whether additives have been used.

MR. WARREN (continues): Three. If it has been prepared, packed, or held under unsanitary conditions.

SALLY: Such as being handled by people with dirty hands--or in places where there are flies, rats, etc.?

MR. WARREN: Exactly. Four. If it is the product of an animal which died other than by slaughter.

ROGER: I had wondered if diseased animals or animals accidentally killed could be sold as food.

MR. WARREN (continues): Five. If the container has any poisonous substance which may make the contents injurious to health. There are other provisions, too, such as those guarding against economic adulteration.

ROGER: For example?

MR. WARREN: Oh, substituting for or leaving out ingredients that ought to be present.

ROGER: Those lawmakers had a good imagination to come up with some of those provisions.

MR. WARREN: Well, I'm afraid there was some justification for each provision. In the past, a few packing houses were not as careful as they should have been.

SALLY: A program like that must cost a lot of money.

MR. WARREN: Yes, it costs money--but the cost is not prohibitive. And as Roger said, the program protects the consumer who, in this case, isn't in a very good position to protect himself. (Telephone rings in background.)

LARRY (from offstage): Telephone, Mr. Warren!

SALLY: Thanks a lot, Mr. Warren. I think all of us need to know more about these laws.

MR. WARREN: You're entirely welcome. Excuse me.

ROGER (turning to face Sally): Did you buy bread? Last week you forgot it.

SALLY: It's in the basket over there.

ROGER: Soup?

SALLY: Yes.

ROGER: Lunch meat?

(Larry re-enters, rearranges display.)

SALLY: That's next on my list. (Picks up packaged luncheon meat.) Larry, this package of liverloaf has "6 ounces" on the label. Was it weighed before or AFTER the wrapping was put on it?

LARRY: That's the weight of the contents. The law we were talking about also contains prohibitions against misbranding.

SALLY: What's that--misbranding, I mean.

LARRY: It means false labeling, for instance.

SALLY: Like giving the wrong weight? Or calling the product something it isn't?

LARRY: That's right.

SALLY: What else does misbranding mean?

LARRY (calling toward storeroom): Mr. Warren! We have another question for you.

(Enter Mr. Warren.)

MR. WARREN: Sure, Larry. What is it?

LARRY: Sally wants to know what misbranding means.

MR. WARREN: Let's see now. Meat or meat products are misbranded, according to the law, if (writes on wrapping paper as before): One. The labeling is false or misleading in any particular. Two. It is offered for sale under the name of another food. Three. It is an imitation of another food, unless it is labeled "imitation." Four. The container is made, formed, or filled so as to be misleading.

ROGER: You mean they even have regulations about the shape of a meat container?

MR. WARREN: If it's misleading, yes. (Continues enumerating)
Five. It fails to contain an accurate statement of the quantity
of contents.

SALLY: That's the one Larry was talking about.

MR. WARREN: Six. It doesn't list the name and place of business of the manufacturer, packer, or distributor.

ROGER: That way the buyer (and the government, too) knows who
is responsible for the labeling.

SALLY: Are there any more ways meat can be misbranded?

MR. WARREN: Yes, but I can't recall all of them at the moment.
I've mentioned some of the most important ones.

ROGER (to Sally): Any more? You can't even remember those he
has already told you about.

SALLY (ignoring Roger): Thanks--again. It's good to know we
can depend on the labels to give us accurate information. (Turning to Roger) Come on, Mr. Know-It-All, it's getting late!

(Roger and Sally leave the counter, walking toward the front of
the store.)

SALLY: One thing I don't understand.

ROGER: Then ask me, and give Mr. Warren a break.

SALLY: All right, I will. Who does the inspecting? It doesn't
seem reasonable to me to expect them to have somebody from the
government at every packing house to inspect all the animals.

ROGER: Oh but they do! At the federally inspected plants, any-
way. Mr. Torrence, who lives over on Maple Avenue, is an inspector for the USDA.

SALLY: Does he inspect pork, too?

ROGER: Of course.

SALLY (who has been glancing at groceries on display as they
walked): Look! pizza! Would you like pizza tonight, Roger?

ROGER: No I wouldn't. We had it for lunch!

SALLY (not greatly embarrassed, but changing the subject):
What if a packing plant operates at night? Is its operation inspected at night, too?

ROGER: Sure. The position of the sun doesn't have anything to
do with it.

SALLY: How about TV dinners tonight?

ROGER: How about steaks tonight?

SALLY: But I was saving them for Sunday, when Mother is coming
to dinner.

ROGER: And when I have to be in Central City for the bowling tournament.

SALLY: Sure. Why else did you think I bought only two steaks?

ROGER: Let's go back and buy two more. I want steak tonight!

(They turn to go back to the meat counter.)

SALLY: Larry, what happens if an inspector finds meat that is adulterated?

LARRY: It is stamped "inspected and condemned" and destroyed for food purposes.

ROGER: Two more T-bones, Larry.

SALLY: And trim off the purple ink, please.

LARRY: Glad to.

SALLY: What happens if meat or meat products are misbranded?

LARRY: Then the item is withheld from the market until it is labeled correctly. But the packer has the right to appeal the decision of misbranding.

SALLY: Can't somebody get around all these requirements by making his own stamp and purple ink--to show that the produce was "inspected and passed"?

LARRY: I guess he could. But it's against the law, and heavy penalties are provided for one who violates this law.

SALLY: What about farmers who slaughter food for their own use? It doesn't seem fair to have them send their animals to the packing plant and go through the inspection process. I really object to that!

LARRY: Hold on! As long as that farmer slaughters animals for exclusive use of his family and his non-paying guests and employees, he is exempt from this law.

ROGER: Come on, Sally. It is getting late.

SALLY: I'm ready to leave. Thanks Larry, and tell Mr. Warren thanks, too.

(She takes package from Larry.)

LARRY: All right. I'll tell him tomorrow. He just went home with a headache.

(Roger and Sally walk toward front of the store and exit. Larry exits to storeroom.)

161

INTERVIEWS

There are times in basic business classes when students can
gather firsthand information by asking questions of parents, rela-
tives who work in business, neighbors, or those with whom they do
business. Since every student has some neighbors who are businessmen, and since every family patronizes several businesses, it
should be easy to use the interview.

The interview provides a means whereby every student can become a part of the class activity. It also affords the opportunity for students to extend their experiences beyond the four walls
of the classroom and into the community.

Some of the topics where interviews would be helpful are:

1. Careers in business.
2. Budgeting and record keeping.
3. Savings and investments.
4. Negotiable instruments.
5. Insurance.

FIELD TRIPS

A well organized field trip can be an unparalleled educational
experience, for there is no vicarious experience that can compare
with seeing things in a natural setting for oneself. The field
trip affords an excellent means of utilizing the business community as a laboratory to supplement classroom experiences. Such
excursions are important for building group morale, motivating
interest, socializing students, broadening observations, and experiencing group planning.

Some suggestions that lead to successful field trips are:

1. The teacher should make the trip himself before deciding
   definitely on it as a class activity.

2. The teacher should make sure that the trip selected
   correlates directly with the topic being studied and
   supplements the text discussion.

3. The teacher should plan cooperatively with the host tour director so that both of them understand each other's objectives and are in complete agreement as to what is to be seen and done.

4. Before the trip the teacher should discuss with the class content information, desirable behavior, dress, and safety precautions.

5. The teacher must clear the date and the trip with the school principal (and department chairman, when such exists).

6. The teacher should arrange to use a school bus when one is available. If cars are to be used, the teacher should provide for an adequate number of adult escorts.

7. The teacher should arrange for a seminar at the place to be visited before the tour begins. (In some instances a follow-up session at the "plant" may be desirable also.)

8. The teacher should divide the group into teams of two so that every student will have a "buddy" who makes sure that he is not lost or left behind.

9. The teacher may be required to ask that students obtain written permission from their parents before they can go on a field trip.

NEWSPAPERS AND NEWS MAGAZINES

One of the primary requisites of any good teacher is that he keep up-to-date, and this is doubly true of the basic business teacher. The daily newspaper is one of the best ways to keep abreast of current developments in the world of business. It is often called a "supplement to the textbook," but, in reality, for most persons it is their "living textbook." The daily newspaper is read by the members of almost every family in this country. It stresses the here and now, and for both teacher and student it is an important source of curriculum enrichment.

Purposes which the newspaper helps to serve when used in basic business classes include:

1. Gathering information about contemporary business problems and issues.

2. Developing an awareness of current happenings on the state and national scene.

3. Encouraging the ability to formulate opinions and to think critically.

4. Building student vocabularies of business and economic terms.

5. Supplementing data with up-to-date factual information and supplying statistical data for use in visuals.

Current events may be used as a lesson activity separate and apart from any particular topic currently being studied, or they may be integrated into regular class discussions. Both of these approaches should be utilized. Current events presentations should be succinct, accurate, and timely. The style used in reporting them is similar to that used by newspaper reporters. The reports should cover.

1. What happened.

2. When and where it occurred.

3. Who was involved.

4. Why it occurred--what brought it about (this may not always be known).

5. Why it is significant.

News magazines are especially valuable in that they select from the myriad of happenings those considered to be the most important. They also give a more comprehensive treatment of events than is usually done by the daily newspaper. Among the best sources of reports on current happenings in the field of business are Newsweek, Time, and U.S. News & World Report. Other magazines that have valuable articles for basic business teachers and classes are Changing Times and Reader's Digest.

COMMITTEE WORK

Socialization among student groups is an inherent phase of teaching in basic business classes. Skill in group processes will be used by students throughout their lives--at work, in clubs, in civic and church activities, and in unions or professional associations of which they are members.

Some of the requisites for effective committee work are:

1. A subtopic or problem that lends itself to the small-group process.

2. An allocation of class time for committees to work.

3. Teacher guidance and coordination.

4. Availability of adequate supplementary reference materials.

5. Flexible furniture and space that enhance group activities.

6. Group chairmen who do not dominate the discussion but rather see that all members of the groups have the opportunity to participate.

7. Understanding on the part of class members of the purposes of committees and positive attitudes toward the group process.

Some suggestions that will aid teachers to assure successful committee activities are to:

1. Hold orientation sessions on how to work in small groups before attempting committee work.

2. Have periodic assessments of committee progress.

3. Prepare schedules for completing assignments.

4. Make sure that committees are small enough to work well together--three to five members.

5. Have an understanding of policies pertaining to work procedures--leaving the room to go to the library, caring for materials housed in the classroom, etc.

6. Vary the method of determining group chairmen--appointed by the teacher, chosen by the class as a whole, selected by the committee members.

7. Work some with individual committees on a rotating basis-- also with chairmen, with secretaries, and any members who need help.

8. Aid committees with locating and evaluating material, organizing their findings, and testing their conclusions.

9. Coach class members on successful and interesting ways of presenting committee reports through interaction among

panel members, the use of props, visuals, and duplicated
sheets covering detailed information, etc.

STUDY GUIDES

A study guide is a combination of outlines, questions, and
vocabulary terms to aid students as they read a part of the textbook or a supplementary booklet. Its contributions lie in focus-
ing attention on important items--ideas, terms, definitions, or
summary statements--and in giving specificity to one's study. The
study guide forces the student to look for something instead of
just read with little or no concentration on what is being read.

Here are two examples of study guides covering the same content material--the supplementary booklet, "Your Social Security,"
which may be obtained from the nearest Social Security office.

WHAT DO YOU KNOW ABOUT SOCIAL SECURITY?

Example A

The basic idea of social security is a simple one: During the years that you work you will pay a small fraction of what you earn to the federal government. The government pools your contributions and those it receives from other workers. When you retire (or should you become disabled) the government pays you money from this sum which it has collected from all workers. <u>The amount you receive each month in the form of benefits is determined by the amount you have paid into the fund.</u>

Should you die, the members of your family will receive payments. The amount of their benefits will be determined by the amount of benefits you would have received.

<u>Monthly Cash Benefits</u>

Your account is credited by quarters of a year--each three-month period. In order to be eligible for benefits you must have paid in for a certain number of quarters. The method of determining this is explained on pages 11 and 12.*

Study the table on pages 16 and 17* of the booklet--it shows how much a worker would receive based on different amounts paid in.

NOTE:

1. How much an individual worker would receive
2. How much a widow would receive
3. How much a child would receive
4. The maximum family payment

---

*Page numbers might vary as future editions of the booklet are revised.

Disability Payments

On page 13* you will learn about:

1. When payments start if you become disabled
2. Minimum coverage needed to qualify
3. Benefits payable to the members of the family of a disabled worker

Family Benefits

Note on pages 16 and 17* the amounts payable to your family.

Work After Retirement

Note on page 20* that if you work after you start receiving retirement payments the amount you receive might be reduced somewhat.

How much can one earn without losing any benefits?

At what age may one earn without losing any of his payments?

Example B

The basic idea of social security is a simple one: During the years that you work you will pay a small fraction of what you earn to the federal government. The government pools your contributions and those it receives from other workers. When you retire (or should you become disabled) the government pays you money from this sum which it has collected from all workers. The amount you receive each month in the form of benefits is determined by the amount you have paid into the fund.

---

*Page numbers might vary as future editions of the booklet are revised.

Should you die, the members of your family will receive payments. The amount of their benefits will be determined by the amount of benefits you would have received.

Read the booklet looking for the answers to the following questions:

1. Who is eligible to participate in the program?

2. At what age may a person begin drawing retirement benefits?

3. At what age may one begin drawing full retirement benefits?

4. At what rate does a worker currently pay social security taxes?

5. On what amount of earnings does one currently pay social security taxes?

6. What is the maximum amount of tax an employee pays in one year?

7. Are the members of the family of a covered disabled worker eligible for benefits?

8. What is the minimum monthly benefit a retired worker may draw?

9. What is the maximum amount a covered worker's family may draw as survivor's benefits?

10. If husband and wife both work and pay social security taxes, would the wife draw more under her own account or her husband's?

11. What amount would one need to invest at 5 percent interest to earn as much as one's family can draw?

12. What fraction of a retired worker's benefit may one's spouse draw?

13. What is the maximum amount that a retired worker and his wife together may draw?

14. How much savings invested at 5 percent would one need to pay him the same amount as he and his wife together may draw?

15. How much is the lump sum death benefit? To whom will it be paid?

16. How much must one pay a household worker during a calendar quarter before he must pay social security tax on the worker's earnings?

17. At what rate do the self-employed persons pay social security taxes?

18. Who may be eligible to receive survivor's benefits in case of a worker's death?

19. How long must one work and pay social security taxes before he (or his family members) would be entitled to any benefit payments?

PANELS AND DEBATES

Most people have had some experience with panel presentations--some have been good, and some, not so good. Panels are another way of permitting a small group to work together as a unit and communicate its ideas to others. In the most effective panels the members give-and-take among themselves rather than "recite" in turn, without interruption. Interruptions are necessary, even though they may be very minor, such as merely asking a question, for they break the routine and help hold the attention of those listening. They help make the presentation truly a panel discussion.

As a general rule, after the panel members have completed their formal presentation, the floor is open for questions and further discussion from the other class members.

Some of the goals of using panels are to:

1. Motivate interest and stimulate student discussion.
2. Encourage and sponsor leadership development.
3. Provide opportunities for the more reserved students to participate "up front."
4. Give variety and change of pace to committee reports.
5. Provoke thinking and give depth to learning.

Debates are more formal than panel discussions. Whereas panels might not require a great deal of preparation, debates do. In addition to formal presentations, debates normally allow for one or more rebuttal presentations on each side. Like panel presentations they should be followed by discussion on the part of other class members, for this broadens and sharpens their interest in the debate proceedings.

Debates:

1. Encourage library research.
2. Give depth and breadth to preparation.
3. Develop team work and cooperation.
4. Encourage respect and tolerance of others' opinions.
5. Teach students to reason and organize their thoughts.

ORAL AND WRITTEN REPORTS

Whereas panels and debates represent group activities, reports, either oral or written, are individual projects. They encourage students to develop initiative and sharpen their research skills. Reports force students to go beyond the textbook in their reading. They cause students to bring together and integrate several skills, such as reading, thinking, organizing, and communicating.

Naturally, those students with limited previous experience in preparing reports will need assistance until they master the techniques. Some teachers prepare brief manuals in which they show illustrative examples for headings, subheadings, outlining, footnotes, bibliographies, etc. It is a good practice to have students who bring oral reports to submit a brief outline and summary in writing for the teacher's future reference. Also, when students bring oral reports, they can make them most effective if they observe some of the suggestions given earlier in connection with committee reports, such as using props, visuals, and written outlines.

SUGGESTED TOPICS FOR PANELS, DEBATES,
OR INDIVIDUAL REPORTS

The American Business System

1. My most important business experience.
2. How today's business differs from "the good 'ole' days."
3. Why advertise?
4. The role of advertising in marketing.
5. The newspaper's contribution to business in this community.
6. How consumers vote in the marketplace.
7. The shortcomings of partnerships.
8. Inflation and our economy.

You as a Consumer

1. When is a bargain not a bargain?
2. Discount stores are a detriment to society and consumers.
3. When I go shopping.
4. How governments aid consumers.
5. The work of the Better Business Bureau.
6. How to avoid legal entanglements.
7. The Legal Aid Society.
8. All contracts should be required to be in writing.

Using Credit Effectively

1. The use of credit is good for business, the government, and consumers.
2. Because I didn't read the small print!
3. Small loan companies should be abolished.
4. The many costs of instalment buying.
5. Why people don't pay their bills.
6. The values of paying cash versus buying on instalments.

Government and Business

1. What John Q. Citizen receives for his tax dollar.
2. The general sales tax should be abolished.
3. How the federal government helps small businesses.
4. The U.S. Postal Service should be self-supporting.
5. The pros and cons of a federal sales tax levied against manufacturers.
6. The federal government should rebate tax money back to the states.
7. Some new government programs we need.
8. The federal government and the national debt.
9. How the government helps the farmers.
10. The government should solve a nation's energy problems.

Business and Labor

1. Arbitration, conciliation, and mediation.
2. The work of the National Labor Relations Board.
3. How labor strikes hurt business, the government, and consumers.
4. Automation and job change.
5. Fringe benefits in labor agreements.
6. Unemployment and occupational retraining.
7. Professional people should organize labor unions.
8. Why we need compulsory arbitration in labor disputes.
9. When and why labor unions began and how they have prospered.

QUESTIONS, ACTIVITIES, AND PROJECTS

1. What is the difference in the nature of student discussion before a topic is studied and after it is studied?

2. What is the difference in a question aimed at appraising one's mastery of facts and one that leads students to share experiences or opinions?

3. When do you answer a student's question that does not pertain to "today's topic," and when do you defer answering it?

4. How would you prepare a class group for a field trip?

5. What specific types of information relating to the world of business can be found in the daily newspaper?

6. What do you consider to be the most important single factor in making committee work most effective?

7. What advantages do study guides have over other types of study stimulators?

8. For each of these topics--"Use of Credit," "Protection Through Insurance," "Business and Labor"--prepare questions to:

    a. Introduce the topic.
    b. Provoke thought.
    c. Test knowledge.
    d. Hold interest.

9. Select two topics from those listed below and suggest titles for dramatic skits suitable for use with them:

    a. Government aids for the consumer.
    b. Savings and investments.
    c. Negotiable instruments.
    d. Taxes as sources of government revenue.

10. Select one of the topics listed under the heading "Interviews" in this chapter and for it prepare an interview format for use by students.

11. Examine several recent issues of your daily newspaper and collect advertisements pertaining to savings accounts. Respond to the following questions:

    a. How do they truly encourage savings?
    b. How much do the rates of interest or dividends paid vary?
    c. Why do they vary?
    d. What types of premiums are offered for opening new accounts?

12. Describe an assignment activity for your students relating to "instalment buying" involving the use of the newspaper.

Classroom creativity may be a function of how well the teacher uses the ideas of others.

CHAPTER 10

Specific Teaching Techniques

Nine topics normally covered in one or more of the basic business subjects are:

1. The American business system.
2. Money and banking.
3. Wise money management.
4. Being a good consumer (wise buymanship).
5. Savings and investments.
6. Economic risks and insurance.
7. The effective use of credit.
8. Government, business, and labor.
9. Contracts.

Included in this chapter are a number of helpful ideas directed to the teacher of basic business subjects. The various suggestions for teaching the nine topics listed above include the following:

1. Guide sheets.
2. Attitude inventories.
3. Ideas for introducing unit topics.
4. Suggested student activities.
5. Case studies.
6. Transparency masters, posters, and bulletin boards.

THE AMERICAN BUSINESS SYSTEM

A. SUGGESTIONS FOR LAUNCHING THE TOPIC

Begin by showing the film, <u>What Is Business</u>? This is a one-reel educational motion picture produced by Coronet Films, Inc., and readily available from most film rental libraries, including college and university film libraries in every state.

It does a splendid job of covering the various types of businesses (production, distribution, and services).

Following the showing of the film, the class members may be led in a discussion of local businesses, classifying them as to their principal functions, or in a discussion of ways that they have utilized the services of various local businesses during the past few days. Thus, the students are immediately drawn into active participation.

The Assignment

1. An assignment that may be utilized is to group the class members into committees and give each committee a specified tack-board area. Each committee is to prepare a bulletin-board exhibit illustrating one of the functions of business (production, distribution, or service).

The number of committees may be increased by dividing production into (a) producing raw materials and (b) manufacturing. Distribution may be divided into (a) trade and (b) transportation or into (a) wholesaling, (b) retailing, and (c) transportation.

Each member is to bring pictures to class to illustrate the different types of activities included in his particular committee's business function. These pictures are turned over to the respective committees. Have on hand various sizes of cardboard or plastic letters (or stencils), sheets of cardboard, construction paper of different colors, and felt pens and coloring pencils for committee use in preparing headings and subheadings. Each committee is responsible for the wording of its captions and for the form and design of its exhibit.

If additional committees are needed, students may be appointed to collect specimens of raw materials produced or articles manufactured in the local community or state.

2. Go to the chalkboard and write the heading "Use of Business Services," and then explain that on your way to school you stopped to purchase gasoline for your car. As you talk, write "bought gasoline" on the chalkboard. Then ask the students to name such things as "listened to the radio, read the newspaper, bought school supplies, wrote a check, turned on electricity, used the telephone, bought lunch, rode a bus," etc.

Occasionally interject other services to broaden the types of categories. If necessary (especially for morning classes), ask the students to include any business services they used the previous evening. By including the things they used when eating breakfast, the production phases will be covered. In the end, the chalkboard will be filled with items, and every phase of business will be included.

The next step is to classify these items into the various types of businesses they represent. Various purchases can be grouped under the retailing of products; other items would fall under manufacturing, transportation, or services. When all the major categories of business are covered, they may be organized further in outline form.

From this point on the procedures and activities described under the first method of launching the topic may be followed.

3. Set a table with a typical breakfast scene. (A card table may be used and a table setting of china and silver for one person.) On the table place an electric toaster, an egg, bread, butter, salt, pepper, cereal, cream, sugar, etc. It is possible to collect all the items needed from your home in ten

minutes and carry them to school in a picnic basket. To make it
even more realistic, place a chair at one side of the table, a
large doll in the chair, and the morning newspaper propped in the
doll's lap. Cover all of this with a luncheon cloth and unveil
only after all students are assembled.

Interest really mounts as the students come into the room.
All want to know "What is under that cloth?"

When the cloth is removed, explain that many persons had a
part in making this breakfast possible. For example, the eggs
and milk might have been delivered to the home directly by the
farmer. From here, let the students offer explanations of where
the bread and other items came from and who had a part in getting
them on the table.

From this activity the students learn in a meaningful way
that business is highly specialized and interdependent and that
transportation plays a significant role. In this simple table
setting all major phases of business are represented.

4. Use an attitude inventory such as the one that follows:

What Is Your Opinion Toward the American Business System?

Directions: Indicate your reaction to each of the following statements by stating whether you (1) agree, (2) partially agree, (3) disagree, or (4) are uncertain. For each statement write one of the words: agree, partially, disagree, or uncertain in the appropriate answer space provided.

1. The government should own and operate the basic industries such as steel production, petroleum refining, and electric utilities. _____

2. A person in business should be permitted to make as much profit as his competition permits. _____

3. Businesses in the United States make too much profit. _____

4. American business should be permitted to operate free of government restrictions. _____

5. The amount a business enterprise can earn should be limited by the government. _____

6. A wage earner's salary should be determined by "the supply and demand" in a particular geographical area. _____

7. "Big business" so dominates the business scene today that the small businessman can no longer compete. _____

8. Basic production industries like steel and petroleum contribute more to our economic system than do those that market finished products. _____

9. The free enterprise system rewards the rich and punishes the poor. _____

10. The earning of a profit is not a sufficient justification for a business to exist. _____

11. The American business system should enable each new generation of workers to enjoy a higher standard of living than their predecessors did. _____

12. The individual proprietorship is the best type of business to be in today. _____

B. SUGGESTED ACTIVITIES

1. Have your students read "The Little Red Hen (Revisited),"
on pages 183-184. (© 1970, NATION'S BUSINESS--the Chamber of
Commerce of the United States. Reprinted from the July issue.)
This is a wonderful illustration that provides an excellent opportunity to introduce and discuss the American business system.

2. Prepare a poster with the caption, "Who Had a Part in
Getting This Article to You?" In the center of the poster place
a picture of some well-known article (or the article itself),
such as a pair of shoes. Below the picture or article print the
statement "Businesses are interdependent." For the following
day's assignment, have the students list all persons responsible
for getting the article into their homes.

Begin the discussion the following day with such obvious suggestions as the farmer who raised the animal, the tannery, the
people who work in the factory where it was produced, the local
retailer, and the truckman who delivered it to the home.

Further discussion, however, should include the banker who
loaned money to the farmer who raised the animal, the various
transportation companies along the way, all those who helped
produce the thread for sewing, the dyes used, the nails, and the
rubber heels. See that the utility services for power and light
are mentioned as well as the men who sweep the floors in the
various factories. In fact, all of the raw materials needed could
not be brought together in one place without using some commercial
means of communication--the telephone, the telegraph, or the
United States mail--perhaps all three.

This activity points out the high degree of specialization
in American business, its diversity, and its interdependence.

3. Ask each student to make a special study of some article
that is produced locally. An outline may be developed that will
guide the students' investigations. The study includes such
topics as the sources of raw materials used, the number of per-

sons employed, the various means of transportation used, the
principal marketing areas, the chief means of advertising, the
organizational pattern, etc.

4. Have each student make a list of local businesses, indi-
cating the products they make (or sell) and listing two other
businesses upon which each firm is dependent. Here is a sample
form.

Local Business	Makes or Sells	Dependent upon Other Business for
Example: Creamery	Butter, Ice Cream, and Milk	Farmer for milk Trucker for milk Electricity for power

5. Appoint a committee to study what would be required to
establish a small store that would sell schoolbooks and supplies--
candy, sandwiches, and soft drinks--and sundry grocery items for
the neighborhood. This committee would report to the class on
the various types of needs (capital, building, stock, equipment,
personnel, etc.) and the problems of getting started, such as
zoning, legal restrictions, license, raising capital, type of
organization to use and why, etc.

6. As a review activity, prepare 10 pairs of matching terms
such as capitalism--profit motive; supply and demand--competition;
and production--gross national product. Play the matching game
on page 185.

7. Use the "Beat the Market" games simulating economic
price determination, published by South-Western Publishing
Company. There are five games and an instructor's manual. There
are three games that relate to this topic:

Game 1--<u>Limited</u> <u>Market</u>

This game introduces the concept of collective buying and selling. A demand team competes against a supply team.

Game 2--<u>Limited</u> <u>Competitive</u> <u>Market</u>

This game introduces the concept of retail buying and selling where buyers purchase items in a given price range for resale on the retail market.

Game 4--<u>Competition</u> <u>or</u> <u>Subsidy</u>?

This game introduces the idea of the free competitive market in which items are bought and sold from a company in competition with many other companies.

8. <u>Market</u>. Have two students role play the purchase of some article, such as a pen, camera, or watch. The clerk has different prices, and the buyer dickers trying to decide which to buy. The clerk gives a "special deal" and discounts a discontinued model by 15 percent, whereupon the purchaser agrees to buy that one and a sale is consummated. This is followed by a discussion as to what made up the market situation:

    a. Buyer and seller.
    b. Product or service.
    c. An exchange.
    d. An agreed upon price.

9. <u>Purchasing</u> <u>Power</u>. Obtain an old issue (18 or 20 years old) of a newspaper or catalogue. Cut out ads showing pictures and prices and place them on the left side of a sheet of paper and place corresponding pictures and prices from a current issue on the right side. For example:

<u>20 Years Ago</u>	<u>Today</u>
Shoes - $ 8.59 Suit - $35.00	Shoes - $32.40 Suit - $89.75

The Little Red Hen (Revisited)

Doug Smith, a British Columbia writer, produced a different version of the children's classic, and Piercell Merchandising Ltd., of Windsor, Ontario, illustrated it.

Once upon a time, there was a little red hen who scratched about and uncovered some grains of wheat. She called her barnyard neighbors and said, "If we work together and plant this wheat, we will have some fine bread to eat. Who will help me plant the wheat?" "Not I," said the cow. "Not I," said the duck. "Not I," said the goose. "Then I will," said the little red hen, and she did.

The wheat grew tall and ripened into golden grain. "Who will help me reap my wheat?" asked the little red hen. "Not I," said the duck. "Out of my classification," said the pig. "I'd lose my seniority," said the cow. "I'd lose my unemployment insurance," said the goose.

Then it came time to bake the bread. "That's overtime for me," said the cow. "I'm a dropout and never learned how," said the duck. "I'd lose my welfare benefits," said the pig. "If I'm the only one helping, that's discrimination," said the goose.

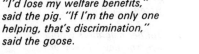

"Then I will," said the little red hen. And she did.

REPRINTED FROM NATION'S BUSINESS, JULY 1970

She baked five loaves of fine bread and held them all up for the neighbors to see. They all wanted some, demanded a share. But the red hen said, "No, I can rest for a while and eat the five loaves myself."

"Excess profits," cried the cow. "Capitalistic leech," screamed the duck. "Company fink," grunted the pig. "Equal rights," yelled the goose. And they hurriedly painted picket signs and marched around the little red hen singing, "We shall overcome," and they did.

For when the farmer came, he said, "You must not be greedy, little red hen. Look at the oppressed cow. Look at the disadvantaged duck. Look at the underprivileged pig. Look at the less fortunate goose. You are guilty of making second-class citizens of them."

"But . . . but," said the little red hen. "I earned the bread."

"Exactly," said the wise farmer. "That is the wonderful free enterprise system; anybody in the barnyard can earn as much as he wants. You should be happy to have this freedom. In other barnyards, you'd have to give all five loaves to the farmer. Here you give four loaves to your suffering neighbors." And they lived happily ever after, including the little red hen, who smiled and clucked: "I am grateful. I am grateful."

But her neighbors wondered why she never baked any more bread.   END

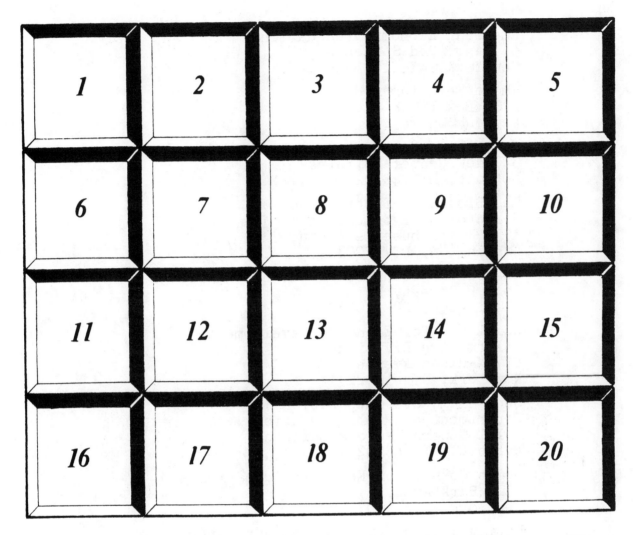

The matching game is played with a board divided into 20
squares large enough for the entire class to see. Ten pairs of
matching terms should be attached to the squares. Each square
should be covered with a numbered piece of paper. The class should
be divided into two teams (or the students may play individually).
The students in turn call two numbers. The papers are lifted from
the two numbers. If they reveal a correct pair of terms, the
papers are removed. If the terms do not match, the papers are re-
placed and the next student chooses two numbers. The players must
remember what is under each number in order to reveal a match and
score a point for their team.

C. SOURCES OF SUPPLEMENTARY MATERIAL

American Economic Foundation
51 East 42nd Street
New York, NY 10017

Amoco Teaching Aids
P.O. Box 1400K
Dayton, OH 45414

Automobile Manufacturers Association
320 New Center Building
Detroit, MI 48202

The Brookings Institution
Director of Publications
1775 Massachusetts Avenue
Washington, DC 20036

Chamber of Commerce of the United States
1615 H Street, NW
Washington, DC 20062

Committee for Economic Development
Information Division
477 Madison Avenue
New York, NY 10022

General Motors Corporation
Department of Public Relations
1-101 General Motors Building
Detroit, MI 48202

Joint Council on Economic Education
1212 Park Avenue
New York, NY 10036

National Association of Manufacturers
Education Department
1776 F Street, NW
Washington, DC 20006

National Industrial Conference Board, Inc.
845 Third Avenue
New York, NY 10022

Phillips Petroleum Company
Phillips Building
Bartlesville, OK 74004

Standard Oil Company of Indiana
Publications and Government Affairs
P.O. Box 5910-A MC3705
Chicago, IL 60680

Texaco, Inc.
135 East 42nd Street
New York, NY 10017

U.S. Department of Labor
Bureau of Labor Statistics
Washington, DC 20212

U.S. Small Business Administration
1441 L Street, NW
Washington, DC 20416

D. TRANSPARENCY MASTERS, POSTERS, AND BULLETIN BOARDS

Sketches appear on succeeding pages.

PRODUCTION

DISTRIBUTION

BUSINESS SERVICES

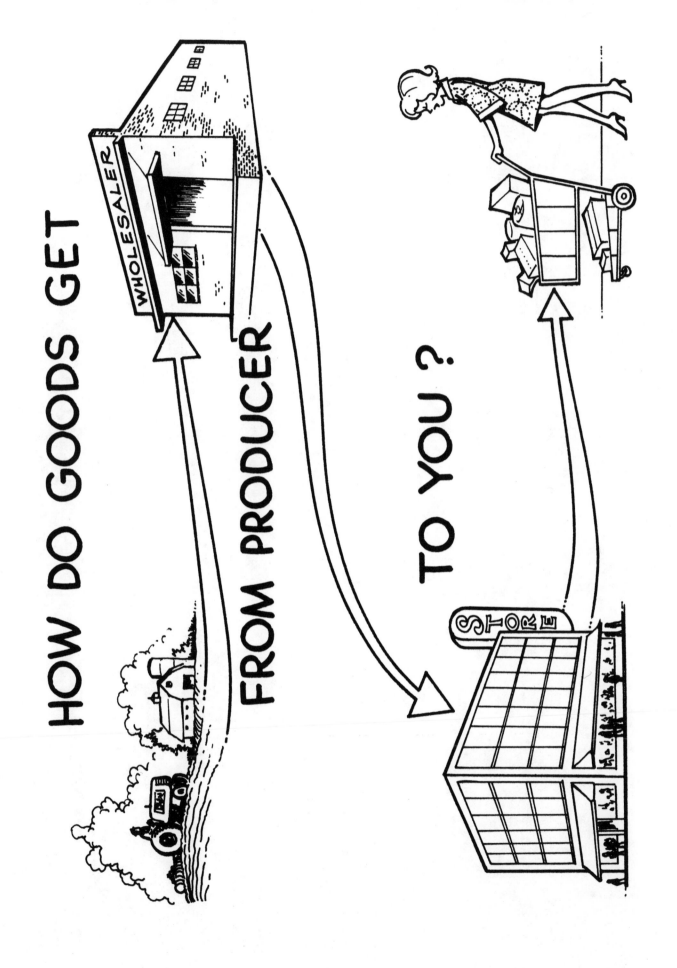

MARKETING CHANNELS

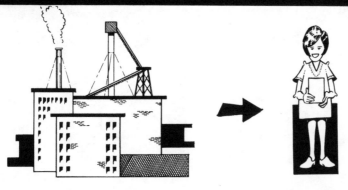

PRODUCER CONSUMER

PRODUCER RETAILER CONSUMER

PRODUCER WHOLESALER RETAILER CONSUMER

MONEY AND BANKING

A. SUGGESTIONS FOR LAUNCHING THE TOPIC

  1. Hold up a worn dollar bill and ask the students to respond to these questions:

      a. Where do you think this dollar bill has been? (Name three places.)

      b. What can I do with it?

      c. If this were yours what would you spend it for?

Follow the class discussion with this account of the travels of a tourist dollar.

Travels of a Tourist Dollar

One community in Tennessee tagged a tourist dollar to find how it traveled about the community for $4\frac{1}{2}$ days. This was the result:

  1. Tourist paid motel bill.
  2. Motel operator paid farmer for eggs.
  3. Farmer bought some gasoline.
  4. Service station operator purchased groceries.
  5. Groceryman paid for his lunch.
  6. Restaurant operator bought tablecloths from department store.
  7. Department store manager bought some first-aid items.
  8. Drug store owner paid for ice for the fountain.
  9. Ice company paid insurance premium.
  10. Insurance agent had shoes repaired.
  11. Shoe store owner paid the doctor.
  12. Doctor paid his electric bill.
  13. Power company bought some window shades from furniture company.

14. Furniture store owner paid fee to attorney.

15. Attorney dropped tourist dollar in church collection plate.

16. Church deposited the dollar in a bank.

2. Hold up a three-ring notebook. Ask: "Who would like to have this notebook?" and "What would you trade me for it?" Finally, "Tomorrow I'll trade this notebook with one of you. Look among your things at home, and see what you have that you'd be willing to trade for it. Maybe you'd better bring more than one thing, and I'll do the same, in case we can't trade even. Let's all have a barter day tomorrow, to see what we can trade." So, tomorrow will be a barter day.

3. Auction off to your class half of a dollar bill; then have the class find out its actual value and follow up with a discussion of what determines the value of money.

4. Give your students some of the early history of the use of different objects for money. For example:

China was the first country to use metals for money, according to an article by John G. Watson, an Englishman, in the May, 1930, issue of The Numismatist. Tcheng, the second emperor of the Tchon dynasty, about 1091 B.C. instituted casting of cubes of gold and rings of bronze to be circulated as money according to their weight. He also authorized the use of silk as money in pieces of specified size.

Moneys used in China include: printed pieces of cardboard, bits of ring-shaped jade from Shensi province, whalebone merchant tokens, small Buddhas used in ancient China, bronze arrowheads from the Wang Meng dynasty, brick tea, and the modern round metal pieces with square holes in the center. Silver dollars with the English words, "One Dollar," on the face were issued in 1885 for use in China, and metal coins shaped like spades, knives, hoes, and shirts were in use several centuries before Christ.

Our own American Indians used bead work, made of shells, called wampum. This was used for money by colonial Americans until

they themselves got to making it so cheaply
that it lost its value as a medium of exchange. Lacking metal or paper money, they
used not only wampum but beaver skins, grain,
and other staples.

Postage stamps enclosed in flat, round
cases, transparent on the top, were used in
Germany, Austria, and France during World War I
to care for the shortage of small change.
A German 1,000,000 mark note and Austrian
bills made of paper and looking like box
labels were also used during the war period.

So far as it can be traced, the motto,
"In God We Trust," dates back to the early
days of the Civil War. Abraham Lincoln's
Secretary of the Treasury, Salmon P. Chase,
received a letter from Rev. M. R. Watkinson
of Ridleyville, Pennsylvania, dated November
13, 1861, urging that some reference to God
appear on coins. Abraham Lincoln was a
profoundly religious man to whom such an idea
would not be offensive. Undoubtedly, the
motto was taken from "The Star Spangled
Banner" in which appear the lines:

"And this be our motto:
In God is our trust."

These words first appeared on coins in 1864,
and in 1955, Congress passed Public Law 140
requiring the inscription "In God We Trust"
to appear on all printed currency as well as
on coins.

B. SUGGESTED ACTIVITIES

1. One of the most successful activities concerns substitutes for money. A substitute would be anything that a person
can use to pay for some article. The check is perhaps the most
familiar so you might use it as an example. Ask the students to
bring other substitutes to class the following day. (Among those
normally brought are: postage stamps, trading stamps, coupons,
money orders, traveler's checks, notes, government bonds, scrip

[such as miners use when trading at the company store], and money telegrams.)

2. As a demonstration have a student apply for a small loan of say $300 for 90 days. You serve as the bank loan officer to make sure the right questions are asked, such as (a) What is your income? (b) What are your fixed expenses? (c) How much is left to apply on repayment of the loan?, all leading up to the big question--How are you going to repay the note when it comes due?

3. Through a role-playing situation show how to open a checking account. Large facsimiles or overhead transparencies of the signature card, deposit slip, and check may be shown by one member of the drama team.

4. Through the use of large facsimiles have a bulletin-board display of the various types of endorsements that may be used when transferring checks to others.

5. Have a display made up of photos of several local banks. Through discussion bring out the differences in the banks (some may be state banks, etc.), the services each renders its depositors, and how they (as a group) serve the community.

6. Ask the question: "How would we carry on business in this community if banks did not exist?" This would involve both personal and company business.

7. Have one of your students who collects coins explain to the class how certain coins come to be valuable and how coin collecting rates as an investment opportunity.

8. Have a committee interview the cashier or loan officer at one of the local banks and report on: "How depositors' money is used for the betterment of the local community."

9. Have a student report on the functions of the Federal Reserve using the pamphlet, "The Four Hats of the Federal Reserve," published by the Federal Reserve Bank of Philadelphia, and the booklet, "The Federal Reserve at Work," published by the Federal Reserve Bank of Richmond, Virginia.

10. Use "A Realistic Bank Project" (pages 200-201) to demonstrate how checks are cleared from one bank to another.

11. Prepare a bulletin board exhibit of the different forms used by local banks.

12. Some banks provide 24-hour service through the automatic handling of deposits and withdrawals in connection with a VISA or Master Charge card. Have a committee investigate this service and report to the class.

13. Have a student report on how VISA or Master Charge works and how "truth-in-lending" affects bank loan procedures.

14. Have two groups of students debate the issue of the "cashless" society. Have one group discuss the issue from the point of view of the banks and business concerns and the other group discuss it from the point of view of the consumer.

A REALISTIC BANK PROJECT

This project involves the establishment of from two to four
banks, each of which consists of no more than seven and no less
than five staff members: namely, a president, a teller, a bookkeeper, an auditor, and a messenger. If the class is large, a
vice-president to assist the president in supervision and an extra
teller, bookkeeper, auditor, or messenger may be necessary.

It is important for the presidents to be respected by the
other members of the class--to be leaders, who will not only understand all the bank processes but who can also inspire cooperation
and help with discipline within their banks. It may be best for
the instructor to appoint the presidents. The rest of the class
and members will become workers and depositors of the banks. Each
bank will meet as a unit and decide who will serve on the other
jobs, letting the members have their choice when possible. At this
time, a distinctive name should be chosen for each bank. At the
meetings, the presidents will conduct the proceedings and keep
order, and everyone should learn more of democratic processes.

Each president should be made to realize that most of the
responsibility for the success of the project rests on his
shoulders. He must see that all work is being done and that it
is being done correctly, that everyone has something to do and is
doing it, that discipline is maintained within his bank, and that
the entire bank is functioning smoothly as an organization. The
bank officials should answer all the questions of the members,
coming to the instructor only when they do not know or cannot
find the answers. Individual members should direct their questions to the president rather than to the instructor.

One deposit slip, one signature card, and five checks are required for each depositor in order to complete each phase of bank
procedure.

Everyone will open an account for $300, using a signature
card and deposit slip. The teller sends the deposit slips through

the bank. If careful inspection is made of this initial entry, many later difficulties can be avoided.

Each person will write and receive five checks for five different amounts drawn on his bank, as shown by the chart on page 202. (This chart will have to be adjusted if less than four banks are established.) First, the payee, then all bank employees, particularly the tellers, inspect each check for correct spelling, correct amounts, and other good checkwriting practices. When each individual has received all five checks, deposit slips are made, the checks are endorsed, and the deposits are taken to the teller of his bank.

From the teller, the checks proceed through the bank, going to the bookkeeper, the auditor, and finally to the messenger, who cancels them. Messengers from all of the banks will meet, exchange checks, adjust balances, and finally return with all checks belonging to their respective banks. These are turned over to the auditor, who starts them back through the bank, deducting them from the customers' accounts. The teller finally receives them and distributes them to the original writers. The bank cycle is now complete.

THE BANK PROJECT CHART

Bank	Students' Names	Write Checks Payable to Students	Amount
1	1 2 3 4 5 6	2, 3, 4, 5, 6 1, 7, 8, 9, 10, 11, 12, 13, 14, 15, 16, 17, 18, 19, 20, 21, 22, 23, 24, 1, 2, 3, 4, 5, 7	$55.25 4.32 11.15 9.49 27.84
2	7 8 9 10 11 12	6, 8, 9, 10, 11 12, 13, 14, 15, 16, 17, 18, 19, 20, 21, 22, 23, 24, 1, 2, 3, 4, 5, 6, 7, 8, 9, 10, 11, 13	$61.71 19.59 12.98 5.00 7.89
3	13 14 15 16 17 18	12, 14, 15, 16, 17, 18, 19, 20, 21, 22, 23, 24, 1, 2, 3, 4, 5, 6, 7, 8, 9, 10, 11, 12, 13, 14, 15, 16, 17, 19	$59.75 1.14 25.35 6.10 13.43
4	19 20 21 22 23 24	18, 20, 21, 22, 23, 24, 1, 2, 3, 4, 5, 6, 7, 8, 9, 10, 11, 12, 13, 14, 15, 16, 17, 18, 24, 19, 20, 21, 22, 23	$48.00 7.69 4.30 33.07 14.45

C. SOURCES OF SUPPLEMENTARY MATERIAL

American Bankers Association
1120 Connecticut Avenue, NW
Washington, DC 20036

FDIC
550 17th Street, NW
Washington, DC 20429

Federal Reserve Bank of Atlanta
Federal Reserve Station
Atlanta, GA 30303

Federal Reserve Bank of Boston
600 Atlantic Avenue
Boston, MA 02106

Federal Reserve Bank of Chicago
Box 834
Chicago, IL 60690

Federal Reserve Bank of Cleveland
P.O. Box 6387
Cleveland, OH 44101

Federal Reserve Bank of Dallas
Station K
Dallas, TX 75222

Federal Reserve Bank of Kansas City
Federal Reserve Station
Kansas City, MO 64198

Federal Reserve Bank of Minneapolis
250 Marquette Avenue
Minneapolis, MN 55480

Federal Reserve Bank of New York
Federal Reserve PO Station
New York, NY 10045

Federal Reserve Bank of Philadelphia
100 N. 6th Street
Philadelphia, PA 19101

Federal Reserve Bank of Richmond
P.O. Box 27622
Richmond, VA 23261

Federal Reserve Bank of St. Louis
P.O. Box 442
St. Louis, MO 63166

Federal Reserve Bank of San Francisco
400 Sansome Street
San Francisco, CA 94120

Publications Services
Division of Administrative Services
Board of Governors of the Federal Reserve System
Washington, DC 20551

D. TRANSPARENCY MASTERS, POSTERS, AND BULLETIN BOARDS

Sketches follow on succeeding pages.

WHO NEEDS A BANK ?

FARMER FRED

TYCOON THOMAS

TEACHER TESSIE

DOCTOR DAN

HOUSEWIFE HAZEL

HOW DO BANKS SERVE CONSUMERS ?

CHECKS & SAVING

SAFE DEPOSIT

WILLS & TRUSTS

LOANS

FOLLOW THE CHECK

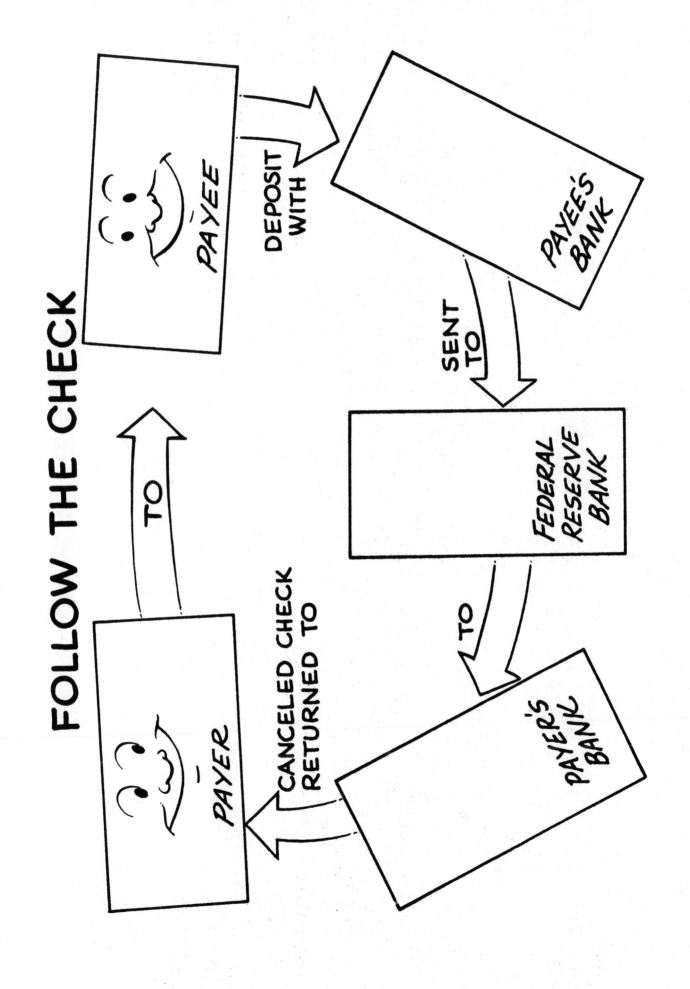

PAYEE

DEPOSIT WITH

PAYEE'S BANK

SENT TO

FEDERAL RESERVE BANK

TO

PAYER'S BANK

CANCELED CHECK RETURNED TO

PAYER

TO

WISE MONEY MANAGEMENT

A. PRETEST

<u>Directions:</u>   Read each statement below carefully. If the state-
ment is true write the word "true" in the blank pro-
vided at the right. If the statement is false write
the word "false."

1. In order to manage money effectively one must
    have goals.   1. _____

2. Effective financial management is dependent
    upon a workable plan.   2. _____

3. Most consumers rate high when it comes to
    their spending habits.   3. _____

4. A budget is essentially a record of a per-
    son's expenditures.   4. _____

5. A budget deals mostly with one's regular
    flexible expenses.   5. _____

6. The best budgets are based on records of
    earlier expenditures.   6. _____

7. Both businesses and consumers need budgets.   7. _____

8. A good budget should be tailor-made to fit
    a particular situation.   8. _____

B. SUGGESTIONS FOR LAUNCHING THE TOPIC

1. Begin this topic by having each class member write answers
to a series of questions. Questions such as those which follow
will give a good background for developing the essentials of a good
money-management plan.

> a. What percentage of all the money you receive (allow-
>   ance, part-time work, etc.) do you spend?
>
> b. What percentage do you save as a regular practice?
>
> c. To what degree can you account for all the money you
>   spent during the past week?   90 percent _____
>   80 percent _____
>   70 percent _____

d. What have you bought during the past three months that you still have (name assets, not expendable items like food, supplies, movies, etc.)?

e. What kind of records do you keep of your cash expenditures?

f. What percentage of each week are you broke? Do you usually spend your money rapidly or apportion it out over the entire week?

g. Do you try to spend a little of each week's income for some tangible article of value?

h. What types of items do you buy with the money you spend?

lunches   _____
movies   _____
gasoline   _____
clothes   _____

i. Do you buy things on the instalment plan?

j. Do you plan how to spend your weekly income or do you just spend it?

k. Do you sometimes borrow from family members or friends? If so how frequently?

l. What rules do you observe when you spend your income?

2. Ask the students to write their definitions of the word "thrift," and below that, their ideas of the key to being thrifty. Compare their answers through group discussion.

3. Supply your class members with a list of advertising commercials and see how many they know. The purpose is to develop interest and provide for 100 percent student participation. (You would need to spend a couple of evenings monitoring your TV and radio programs in order to prepare your list.) Present to your students the advertising quiz, on page 214, which includes a list of slogans.

4. As a follow-up activity discuss the influence advertising has on consumers.

5. Divide your class into groups and ask each group to invent a product that has never been fully marketed in your community, one within the realm of reality. One class group in one situ-

ation suggested an instant cola in tea bag form; another a ciga-
rette with built-in match tip to avoid matches or lighters.

6. Have your students prepare a paper giving an outline for
a full marketing plan for the product suggested in item 5, including topics such as slogans, jingles, promotional activities, store
displays, composition, price, etc., and a lay-out for a magazine
ad, a billboard display, and one radio commercial.

Advertising Quiz

Place a pad of paper and a pen near your television. Keep a record of the commercials you hear and prepare a list to be used as an advertising quiz, like the following. A section can also be added for local commercials of two types: (a) long-term organization/product advertisements, and (b) short-term promotional advertisements.

The following are various slogans, tunes, and personalities for products advertised daily in the southern United States. Fill in the brand name of the product for each. If you were able to remember the slogan because it is part of a tune, write a "T" after the brand name. If you don't know the brand name, then put the type of product simply to show you have retained something.

Slogans

1. Bring out the _____ and bring out the best.   1._____
2. _____ is one-quarter cleansing cream.   2._____
3. Poppin' fresh dough.   3._____
4. The slow ketchup.   4._____
5. My wife, I think I'll keep her.   5._____
6. Breakfast of champions.   6._____
7. _____ is the savings store.   7._____
8. Where America shops.   8._____
9. _____ lets the good times roll.   9._____
10. _____, for the times of your life.   10._____
11. Don't get dressed without it.   11._____
12. Do you know me?   12._____
13. Give your watch a new twist with _____.   13._____
14. Weekends were made for _____.   14._____
15. You, you never looked so good.   15._____
16. We do it all for you.   16._____
17. King of beers.   17._____

18. Don't squeeze the _____. 18._____
19. When you're out of _____, you're out of beer. 19._____
20. Good things are goin' on _____. 20._____
21. C'mon, c'mon, c'mon and have a _____ day. 21._____
22. It doesn't give you medicine breath. 22._____
23. The sign of the cat. 23._____
24. Square meal, square deal at _____. 24._____
25. 90%, acid-neutralized coffee. 25._____
26. America's shirt company. 26._____
27. Who has the blimp? 27._____
28. The superstar in rent-a-car. 28._____
29. You asked for it, you got it. 29._____
30. Bacon makin' people. 30._____

Personalities

31. Mrs. Olsen 31._____
32. Aunt Blue Belle 32._____
33. Rosie of Rosie's Diner 33._____
34. Mr. Whipple 34._____
35. Mavis the Waitress 35._____
36. Cora 36._____
37. Sarah of Tucker Inn 37._____
38. Morris 38._____
39. Tony the Tiger 39._____
40. Elsie the Cow 40._____
41. A tree full of elves 41._____
42. Brother Dominic 42._____
43. Mr. Cholesterol 43._____
44. The bowl that says, "butter." 44._____
45. Bill Cosby 45._____

C. SUGGESTED ACTIVITIES

1. Have each class member interview his mother and one
neighbor to learn whether they use a budget to govern their
expenditures. If a budget is used have the student ask the
person:

        a. What is the secret of making a budget work?
        b. What are the fixed expenditures?
        c. What are some flexible expenditures?

2. Supply the class members with a line graph showing the
Consumer Price Index for a recent period of time. Lead a discussion on the reasons for the current trend in the index--what
prices are increasing or decreasing: food, appliances, fuel,
housing, etc.

3. One aspect of good financial management is the keeping
of important papers. Have the class members ask their parents
what kinds of important papers should be kept and where they
should be kept. Compile their findings. The list should include
cancelled checks, insurance policies, deeds, birth certificates,
stocks, bonds, records of large furniture or clothing purchases,
inventories of furniture and clothing, etc.

4. Ask the class members to prepare, with the aid of their
parents, inventories of all of their household furnishings. The
records should include date of purchase, cost, and where purchased. (Where families already have such inventories they may
be updated, or the student may prepare one for the things he owns.)

5. Ask class members to explain how advertising is related
to money management.

D. SOURCES OF SUPPLEMENTARY MATERIAL

        Advertising Council, Inc.
        825 Third Avenue
        New York, NY 10022

American Advertising Federation
1225 Connecticut Avenue, NW
Washington, DC 20036

Council of Better Business Bureaus, Inc.
1150 17th Street, NW
Washington, DC 20036

Household Finance Corporation
Prudential Plaza
Chicago, IL 60601

E. TRANSPARENCY MASTERS, POSTERS, AND BULLETIN BOARDS

   Sketches appear on succeeding pages.

DO YOU SPEND YOUR $ WISELY ?

SUZY
A
L
E
S

NANCY
NECESSITY

BETTY
BUDGET

QUEENIE
QUALITY

SHOWERS OF BUYING DECISIONS

WHAT TO BUY

CATALOG SALE

WHERE TO BUY
A B

WHEN TO BUY
JAN. FEB. MARCH

QUALITY TO BUY

BUDGETING HELPS YOU

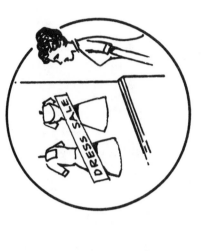

PUT FIRST THINGS FIRST

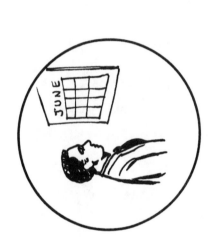

MAKE WISE CHOICES

$ INCOME $
INCOME
INCOME $

LIVE WITHIN INCOME

LOOK AHEAD

BUILD RESERVE

HOW TO MAKE YOUR BUDGET WORK

1 *GIVE IT A FAIR TRIAL*

---

2 *CHANGE ESTIMATES IF NECESSARY*

---

3 *KEEP RECORDS SIMPLE*

$$\begin{array}{r} 1 \\ +1 \\ \hline 2 \end{array}$$

---

4 *HAVE A WELL-BALANCED BUDGET*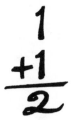

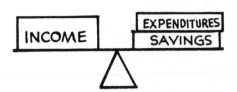

---

5 *HAVE A LITTLE OIL (EMERGENCY FUND) TO MAKE IT WORK*

BEING A GOOD CONSUMER

(Wise Buymanship)

A. SUGGESTIONS FOR LAUNCHING THE TOPIC

1. Select two items of several different types of goods, such as two ties, two blouses, two small transistor radios, two pens, or two brief cases. One item of each pair should cost considerably more than the other.

Label one item in the pair "A" and the other "B" and place on a table. Specify a certain amount of money that each student can spend (the amount to depend on the number of articles used and the value of each). Allow more than enough money to cover all of the cheaper items. Have each student examine and select one item from each set.

After the students have made their selections, give them the prices of all items and have them note the prices of the ones they chose. Have each student total the cost of all the items he selected.

Ask the student whose total came the closest to the dollar figure allowed to explain to the class what he looked for in deciding on these particular items.

This will lead into a discussion of the principles of wise buying.

2. Have students bring labels from canned goods to class. Determine what information is provided on the different labels. Construct an "ideal label" combining information from all labels.

3. Bring to class newspaper ads that show the regular price and the sale price of different types of goods such as shoes, clothing, furniture, or appliances.

Point out that there are various "right times" to buy; when goods are priced at their regular prices; when they are on sale on anniversary dates; and when they are on sale at the end of the season. Ask students to suggest the advantages and disadvantages

225

of buying at different times. (For example, if one buys highly fashionable clothing at the end of the season, the style very likely will change before the next year.) Continue the discussion to bring out other factors to be observed in buying in addition to the right time to buy. (For example, buying the proper quantity and quality to meet specific needs, buying for cash or credit, etc.)

4. Have students bring to class a current issue of the local paper that contains the grocery ads. Prepare a list of a number of items which are being sold as "specials" in one or more stores. (Obtain the regular price for each item beforehand.) Have the students determine the difference in the total cost of all items being bought at their regular prices versus their being bought at the special prices.

Raise the question as to whether it is worthwhile to go to several stores in order to save the sum of money saved by doing so. (Other factors that enter into this discussion are the cost of extra miles of driving, the value of the shopper's time, the investment of money in staple food items one won't use right away, and the amount of storage space one has at home.)

B. SUGGESTED ACTIVITIES

1. Have a committee visit an independent retail store and a discount house that handles the same type of merchandise and select identical or similar articles and compare prices. Explain what services one store gives that justifies its charging higher prices.

2. Have a speaker from the local Better Business Bureau or other consumer service association explain the types of services available from that organization.

3. Have a committee of two students interview a department manager at one of the local department stores to learn about

problems that grow out of selling goods on credit, such as unnecessary return of goods, etc.

4. Have each student bring to class some article (paint brush, woolen sweater, portable radio, TV, or record player) and explain to the class how to care for the article properly in order to receive maximum service from it.

5. Prepare a display of colorful pictures of a variety of items such as a dress, TV set, shoes, bicycle, boat, radio, candy bar, or sandwich. Ask the class for which of these articles would it pay to "shop around" and why?

6. Prepare a list of 20 items and have students group them as to whether they can normally be purchased: direct from the manufacturer, at the wholesale price, for free delivery, by mail order, with trading stamps, on 90-day credit without paying a carrying charge, or on instalment credit.

7. Have two students attend an auction and report on their observations.

8. Have each student pretend he is buying two articles during a given period of time (to include a weekend) that are being offered for sale at reduced prices by stores in your local community. The idea is to see who can save the most money by making the two purchases.

9. Give as a special assignment for students to find out how many different kinds of articles can be obtained from vending machines. (At some motels quite a variety of goods is available.)

10. Have a committee determine what kinds of middlemen (brokers, etc.) live and work in your community. (Eliminate the wholesaler who takes possession of the goods.) Ask what kind of consumer protection is available if one purchases from them.

11. Supply your class with a chart that shows the percentage of the family income which is spent for different items (housing, medical care, transportation, etc.) for different income levels. As a written assignment, have each student select the income level that fits his family situation and, in cooperation with his parents,

indicate which percentages differ from those shown in the chart and by how much.

12. Have each student develop a list of spending rules that will help make a person a wise shopper.

13. Have students write answers to these questions concerning their legal rights as a buyer.

    a. Where is the nearest Legal Aid Society, Better Business Bureau, or Small Claims Court that offers help to consumers?

    b. When should contracts be in written form?

    c. What warranty can one expect when buying mechanical goods with moving parts?

    d. For what period of time should a warranty on a refrigerator be good? What does it cover?

    e. What are one's rights regarding the receipt through the mail of unordered merchandise?

    f. To whom can one appeal if a merchant appears to be guilty of using misleading advertising?

14. Use the Basic Kit on Consumer Advertising put out by Procter and Gamble Educational Services. The kit consists of a 32-page teacher's manual, a 16-page teacher idea piece, a 20-minute sound filmstrip (in color), and fifty 8-page student booklets.

15. Use the Consumer Series Filmstrips available from Association Films (600 Grand Avenue, Ridgefield, NJ 07657). The titles of the strips are:

Our Role as Consumers
Consumers in the Market
Consumers in Action

C. SOURCES OF SUPPLEMENTARY MATERIAL

Better Business Bureau in your local community.
Bureau of Consumer Affairs in your state government.

228

Consumer Information Center
Pueblo, CO 81009

Consumers Union
P.O. Box 1000
Orangeburg, NY 10962

Delta Pi Epsilon National Office
Gustavus Adolphus College
St. Peter, MN 56082

Household Finance Corporation
Prudential Plaza
Chicago, IL 60601

J. C. Penney Company, Inc.
Educational Relations Department
1301 Avenue of the Americas
New York, NY 10019

Journal of Consumer Affairs
American Council on Consumer Interests
238 Stanley Hall
University of Missouri
Columbia, MO 65201

Sears, Roebuck, and Company
Sears Tower
Chicago, IL 60684

D. TRANSPARENCY MASTERS, POSTERS, AND BULLETIN BOARDS

Sketches appear on succeeding pages.

WHAT GOVERNMENT AGENCIES AID THE CONSUMERS

FOOD & DRUG ADMINISTRATION

BUREAU OF STANDARDS

FEDERAL BUREAU OF AVIATION

INTERSTATE COMMERCE COMMISSION

SECURITIES & EXCHANGE COMMISSION

NO. 303 CAN
INGREDIENTS
Apricots in a Syrup
of Water, Sugar, and
Corn Sweetener

PACKED IN
U.S.A.

Quality
★ ★ ★ ★ ★
APRICOTS
IN HEAVY SYRUP

Net Wt. 17 oz. 482 Grams

SAVINGS AND INVESTMENTS

A. HOW MUCH DO YOU KNOW ABOUT SAVING AND INVESTING?

Use the following as a guide sheet for use with this topic.

1. When you start a savings program, is the elimination of luxury spending your first step?

2. When you add up your annual savings, should you include what you have paid on the principal of your mortgage?

3. Are increases in the cash values of your life insurance policies a form of savings?

4. As protection against inflation, which are better, common stocks or bonds?

5. Do banks usually pay a higher return on savings than savings and loan associations pay?

6. Are your dollars safer in corporation bonds than in common stocks?

7. Does diversity rank ahead of safety when choosing one's investments?

8. Do corporate bonds yield a higher rate of interest than government bonds?

9. Is it possible to purchase stocks in small amounts every month?

10. Is it better to try to buy stocks when the market is low than to buy at regular intervals regardless of price?

11. How do mutual funds work? What is meant by the loading factor?

12. If you buy shares in a mutual fund, do you get free money management?

13. Is a three-year upward trend in earnings an indication that a company's stock is a good investment?

14. What is the chief advantage of government bonds as an investment?

15. If you are investing for growth, what type of investment should you make?

16. When are bonds a better investment than common stocks?

17. What causes fluctuations in the stock market and how are stock prices determined?

B. SUGGESTIONS FOR LAUNCHING THE TOPIC

1. Use an attitude inventory such as the following:

What Is Your Opinion About Savings and Investments?

Directions: Indicate your reaction to each of the following statements by stating whether you (1) agree, (2) partially agree, (3) disagree, or are (4) uncertain. For each statement write one of the words: agree, partially, disagree, or uncertain in the appropriate answer space provided.

1. Only persons who can afford it should have savings accounts. _____

2. A commercial bank is the best place to have a savings account. _____

3. The percent of interest one earns on savings is more important than being systematic and regular with one's plan. _____

4. Buying a home is the best investment a young married couple can make. _____

5. Bonds are better investments than common stocks. _____

6. The frequency with which interest is compounded is more important than the rate of interest earned. _____

7. Safety is the prime consideration when choosing investments. _____

8. Purchasing a home should be undertaken before making other types of investments. _____

9. The rate of return on an investment is more important than being able to cash it quickly. _____

10. Mutual funds are better for most persons than buying stocks in individual companies. _____

11. A person should have a savings account and own life insurance before considering other types of investment. _____

12. Considering all factors it is cheaper to own
one's home than to pay rent on comparable
housing.   _____

   2. Ask the class "What types of things might a family want
to buy that cost more than they might be able to spare from their
bank account?" (Examples: furniture, appliances, an automobile,
a TV set, a vacation, a home.) Then ask "How would a family meet
this type of need?" (Answers might include borrowing or buying
on the instalment plan but would also include withdrawing from
savings.) After listing these on the board you can suggest that
there are other reasons for savings too, such as meeting emergen-
cies such as illness, accidents, and unemployment.

   3. Bring to class newspaper ads showing the different rates
of interest paid by local banks, savings and loan associations,
etc. Display these on the tack board. Raise the question: "If
I had some money I wanted to put to work earning interest which
of these would you suggest I use?" This will naturally bring
up the question of the different factors that enter into such a
decision: rate of interest, frequency of compounding, minimum
deposit required, length of time money must remain on deposit,
ease of depositing and withdrawal, whether it is insured, etc.

   4. Have a display on the tack board of colorful pictures
of a TV set, an automobile, a vacation scene, etc. Ask the class
how a person would pay for any of these. Sort out the suggestion
of savings in order to buy it and proceed as in item 2.

C. SUGGESTED ACTIVITIES

   1. As a follow-up activity growing out of the launching
activity number 3, have a committee of two or three students
visit the local businesses to learn the answers to the questions
raised in that activity.

2. Secure copies of the booklet, "How to Invest," published and distributed by Merrill Lynch et al. Study these booklets as a class project.

3. Secure copies of the booklet, "You and the Investment World," from the New York Stock Exchange and study by appointing committees, or use as a class project.

4. Have students bring to class the stock market report from the local paper. Explain the various columns and figures so they can read this report. Have each student select specific stocks to watch for a period of two or three weeks. In some cases, have the students assume a stock purchase of a given amount of money and at the end of the semester determine who made the best purchase.

5. Check to see if the parents of any of your students are members of a local investment club. Such a person, or a representative from a local brokerage firm would make a good speaker for your class.

6. Ask a local realtor to discuss the merits of home ownership versus renting with your class.

7. Obtain copies of a government bond, a corporation bond, and a stock certificate for examination by your students. Have the students determine the pertinent information shown on each.

8. As a review, complete the "Savings and Investments Chart" on page 240, as a class activity.

9. As a review activity, play the matching game using the savings and investments terms and definitions on page 241, following the directions on page 185.

10. As a review activity, have the students work the jigsaw puzzle on page 242.

11. Introduce the case situation "Investing in a Home" on page 243 and have the students answer the questions to the puzzle.

12. Have the class unscramble the words in the "Word Scramble" game on page 244.

13. Display two different homes above the chalkboard:

   Ask the class members if they would prefer to buy a home or to rent one and why. List the advantages of each on the board below each home.

   14. Use Game 3--<u>Competitive Exchange Market</u>--in the "Beat the Market" series of simulation games published by South-Western Publishing Company. This game deals with the buying and selling of common stocks. The game simulates buyers and sellers who seek to make transactions through their respective brokers.

SAVINGS AND INVESTMENTS CHART

Type	Amount to Invest	Degree of Liquidity	Rate of Return	Degree of Safety	Who Invests	When
Fixed Dollar Investments Savings Accounts						
U.S. Savings Bonds						
Life Insurance						
Municipal Bonds						
Corporation Bonds						
Common Stocks						
Home						
Real Estate (Land)						

240

THE MATCHING GAME

1. The most important reason for saving

2. Representing part ownership of a corporation

3. When an investment sells for far more than it cost

4. An investment that can be opened for $1.00

5. Putting savings to work

6. A poor place to keep one's savings

7. Readily convertible into cash

8. A savings plan operated by the federal government

9. The storing up of purchasing power

10. The amount a share of stock or a bond is worth

Security

Stock certificate

Capital gain

Savings account

Investing

Under the bed

Liquid assets

United States savings bond

Saving

Market value

THE JIGSAW PUZZLE FOR REVIEW

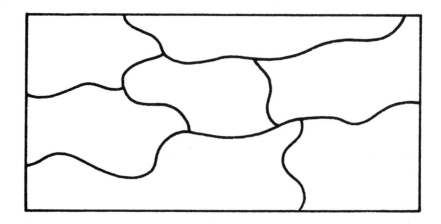

A sheet of cardboard is cut out in pieces that may be fitted together. An outline of the various pieces is drawn on a second sheet of cardboard. Statements have been written on the jigsaw pieces which are handed out to students. If the piece <u>fits</u> <u>in</u> <u>the</u> <u>puzzle</u>, that answer is correct. If it does not fit, the answer is not correct.

For example, using "savings accounts" as the topic for our illustration, the following statements would be written on the individual pieces:

<u>Those</u> <u>that</u> <u>fit</u>:
1. Joint ownership possible
2. Fixed rate of return
3. Liquid investment
4. Convenient way to save
5. Can invest small amounts
6. Insured against loss
7. Fixed-dollar investment

<u>Those</u> <u>that</u> <u>do</u> <u>not</u> <u>fit</u>:
1. Regulated by Federal Reserve System
2. Run by the government
3. High degree of risk
4. Fluctuates with the market

The seven statements on the left fit and complete the puzzle. The statements on the right are written on irregular shaped pieces that will not fit into the puzzle outline.

CASE SITUATIONS

Investing in a Home

The topic was introduced by explaining that Carolyn's mother and father were planning to build a new home. It was also brought out that the initial decisions had already been made, such as the decision to build a home rather than buy one already built, and they had decided on the type of home they wanted. Since the initial decisions had been reached, the question was posed to the students: "What factors should Carolyn's parents consider when finding the building site?" Each factor should represent part of a puzzle. When all the factors have been considered, we will have a complete puzzle. However, if any of these factors has not been considered, then Carolyn's parents might find themselves in an awkward situation. (The factors have been written in question form on the puzzle parts. As students name each of them, the teacher should put up part of the puzzle.)

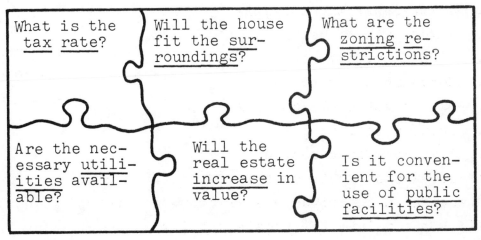

WORD SCRAMBLE

Advantages of Home Ownership

Describe a case situation where a young married couple wants
to know the advantages of owning a home over renting. Ask the
class to unscramble the words which name these advantages. Under
the scrambled word is the advantage of home ownership.

GIASNSV	SAVINGS
BILIYTAST	STABILITY
CRUTIESY	SECURITY
GSREPTIE	PRESTIGE
PRIMNEMTOVES	IMPROVEMENTS
FITONILAN	INFLATION
DECTIR AITGRN	CREDIT RATING

These scrambled words are placed over the correct statements
until they are correctly unscrambled. Then they are removed and
the answer statement is revealed.

A. SOURCES OF SUPPLEMENTARY MATERIAL

American Stock Exchange
86 Trinity Place
New York, NY 10006

Business International Corporation
1 Dag Hammarskjöld Plaza
New York, NY 10017

            or

1625 Eye Street, NW
Washington, DC 20006

Dow Jones & Company, Inc.
Educational Service Bureau
P.O. Box 300
Princeton, NJ 08540

Household Finance Corporation
Prudential Plaza
Chicago, IL 60601

Merrill Lynch, Pierce, Fenner & Smith, Inc.
One Liberty Plaza
New York, NY 10006

National Association of Securities Dealers, Inc.
1735 K Street, NW
Washington, DC 20006

New York Stock Exchange
School and College Relations
11 Wall Street
New York, NY 10005

U.S. Securities and Exchange Commission
Office of Consumer Affairs
Washington, DC 20549

B. TRANSPARENCY MASTERS, POSTERS, AND BULLETIN BOARDS

Sketches appear on succeeding pages.

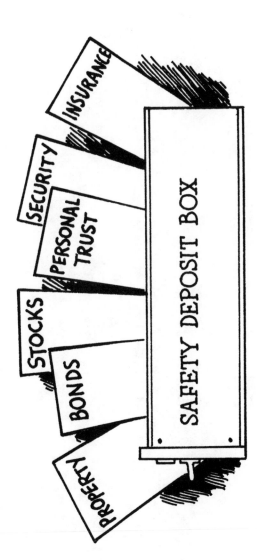

SAVE FOR

BOAT

CAR

HOME

EDUCATION

WEDDING

BY INVESTING IN

INSURANCE

SECURITY

PERSONAL TRUST

STOCKS

BONDS

PROPERTY

SAFETY DEPOSIT BOX

SAVINGS

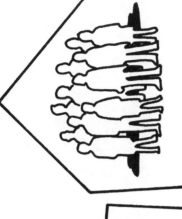

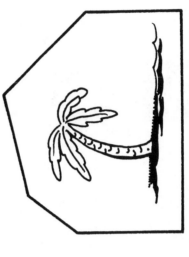

1ST. NAT'L BANK

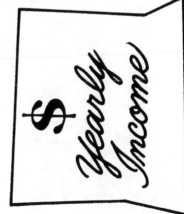

$ Yearly Income

· BANK ACCOUNTS · SAVINGS & LOAN · GOVERNMENT BONDS · CREDIT UNIONS ·

· ANNUITIES · SOCIAL SECURITY · PENSION & RETIREMENT ·

ECONOMIC RISKS AND INSURANCE

A. SUGGESTIONS FOR LAUNCHING THE TOPIC

1. Most textbooks discuss automobile insurance as the first subtopic when presenting insurance. Automobile insurance may be introduced through role-playing situations such as the local happening example described in Chapter 3, pages 42-43. Use this dramatization to launch your discussion of automobile insurance.

2. Continue by explaining that the cost of automobile insurance is not always the same. The variations in cost depend on:

        a. The driving record of the driver
        b. The age of the driver
        c. The type of insurance coverage carried
        d. The type, model, and age of the car
        e. The place the driver lives (urban or rural), etc.

These should be written on the chalkboard as they are discussed, or they could be written on flip-chart paper or on strips to be used on a flannel board.

The next step would be to point out that the premium may be lowered if the driver can qualify for any of the five discounts given. A strip of poster board should cover the name of each discount until it is discussed.

HOW TO QUALIFY FOR REDUCED RATES
1. SAFE DRIVER DISCOUNT
2. DRIVER EDUCATION DISCOUNT
3. COMPACT CAR DISCOUNT
4. TWO OR MORE CARS DISCOUNT
5. FARMER DISCOUNT

3. Dramatization for introducing homeowners insurance.

Have students present a dramatic skit describing events that would result in economic losses if they were not covered by insurance.

The following script magnifies the situation in such a manner as to capture everyone's attention.

A DAY IN THE LIFE OF BONNIE AND CLYDE

Clyde has returned home from a business trip, and Bonnie is driving home after meeting him at the airport. The following conversation takes place during the car ride.

CLYDE: How have things gone today?
BONNIE: Oh, about as usual (pause). Well, Rover did bite the mailman this morning.
CLYDE: Oh no! Did it hurt him--the mailman?
BONNIE: Yah, kinda--blood everywhere--yuk! They took him to the hospital.
CLYDE: Anything else happen?
BONNIE: Oh yes! We had a terrific windstorm--and you know the garage which you planned to paint this weekend? WHOOSH! FLAT ON THE GROUND!
(Bonnie gives a turn signal.)
CLYDE: Say, why did you turn there? You went by our street!
BONNIE: Oh, we don't live there anymore since the house caught on fire today. We're living in this (CRASH) motel.
CLYDE (with despair and a great deal of contempt): Bonnie, why did you drive into the motel? Couldn't we have walked in like other people do?
BONNIE: Must you always be so conventional?

After the dramatization, discuss possible economic losses and the various types of homeowners policies available. Relate the losses in the dramatization to coverages of the homeowners policy.

Make charts showing:

Property Coverages	Amount of Coverage
Dwelling	80 percent of full value
Appurtenant private structures	10 percent of dwelling
Unscheduled personal property	50 percent of dwelling
Additional living expenses	20 percent of dwelling

Liability Coverages

Personal liability
Medical payments
Physical damage to property of others

4. Introduce the topic of life insurance with a tack board or flannel-board presentation using large letters cut out to spell--L I F E--featuring the four types of life policies:

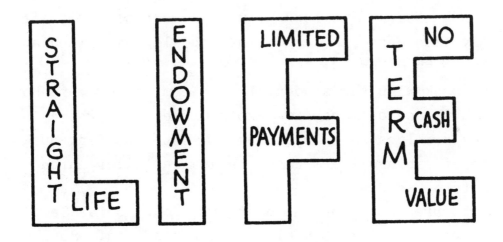

B. SUGGESTED ACTIVITIES

1. Have students bring to class pictures from magazines and/or stories from the newspaper that illustrate or relate to economic risks that may be covered through insurance. Prepare a montage with a separate section for each type of insurance-- auto, property, life, etc.

2. Ask students to prepare inventories of their clothing and other assets to be placed in the family safety deposit box. If the family does not have one for its furniture and appliances these may also be prepared. Use a form such as the following:

Article	Date Purchased	Description	Cost

3. Ask students to look around the school and their homes to see if any fire hazards exist. They should take immediate steps to eliminate said hazards.

4. Check with the students to determine how many homes are equipped with one or more fire extinguishers and where in the homes they are located. Appoint a committee to find out the kinds and costs of extinguishers that are available for purchase locally and report to the class.

5. Secure copies of the booklet, "Your Social Security," from the local or nearest Social Security office. Supply class members with a guide sheet such as those illustrated in Chapter 9, which are based on this booklet.

6. Have a committee of students investigate the types of insurance carried on various types of government property in the community--schools, court house, highway garage, etc.

7. Have a representative from the Blue Cross Association in your community to explain how the Blue Cross-Blue Shield plan works.

8. From a local insurance agent secure comparative costs of

258

various kinds of auto or property insurance showing how they differ in selected locations representing varying degrees of risk.

9. Secure illustrated brochures dealing with homeowners insurance and discuss the different kinds of coverage included with the various homeowners policies (A, B, C broad form, etc.).

10. Using cash values after 5, 10, 15, and 20 years for different types of policies, point out how a person can carry life insurance protection and receive a return of all his premiums paid at the end of a given number of years. (This period of time varies with different types of policies--straight life, limited payment, and endowment.)

11. Prepare four hypothetical family case situations and have students, using the booklet, "Your Social Security," figure out the amount of benefits the family might receive.

12. Use the case situation, "Benefits of Social Security," on page 260 as the basis of a class discussion.

13. Have the class work the crossword puzzle concerning insurance on page 261. (Solution is found on page 262.)

Benefits of Social Security

John Williams started working right after graduation from high school for the American Manufacturing Company in his home town. When he received his first pay check he found that there was a deduction for social security taxes that he had not planned on.

John did not understand why he had to pay social security taxes when he was just 18 years old. He had heard his grandparents talk about getting their social security checks each month and he knew his father paid social security tax and planned on it as income for his retirement in a few years. It did not seem fair to John that he had to pay social security taxes while he was young and so far from retirement.

John showed his deduction slip to his father and asked why the social security tax was taken out of his check and what good was it to him when retirement was so far away.

If John asked you these questions, what would you tell him about the advantages there are in having social security?

Answers are:

1. Lack of need to support Grandpa
2. Benefits in case of disability
3. Benefits to wife and children in the near future
4. Knowledge that when you are in Grandpa's place, you will receive old-age benefits
5. Benefits of "Medicare"

ACROSS

1. Type of life insurance that amounts to an insured savings plan.

2. The least expensive type of permanent protection in life insurance is _____ life.

4. A person who has insurance.

8. Disability insurance pays for loss of _____.

9. Hospital, surgical, and _____ insurance are often called basic health coverage.

11. Type of life insurance policy that protects for a given period of years.

13. A provision that under certain conditions an insurance policy will be kept in full force by the company without the payment of premiums is called a _____ of premium.

15. A family income _____ may be added to a straight life policy.

16. An insurance contract.

17. Life Underwriters Associations are organizations of insurance _____.

22. Having insurance gives one a feeling of _____.

23. Insurance companies help finance home and apartment buildings by investing in _____.

24. A means of sharing risks.

25. A permanent life insurance policy has a _____ value, which the policyholder may borrow against.

26. A double indemnity policy pays double when death results from _____ means.

DOWN

1. Type of risk that may cause financial loss.

3. Type of insurance plan often provided by a wage earner's company.

5. The insurance company puts money to work in _____.

6. The two types of personal insurance are life and _____.

7. The type of insurance in which premiums are paid for a set number of years but protection lasts for life is called _____ payment.

10. Type of insurance that protects against the claims of other people if the insured person should injure them or damage their property.

12. Charges for insurance are known as premium _____.

14. Amount paid for insurance.

18. Overhead insurance is a type of _____ health insurance.

19. Chance of losing something of value.

20. Surgical _____ insurance is a type of health insurance.

21. All permanent life insurance has _____ values. This means that insurance protection need not be given up to get the use of cash in an emergency.

Solution

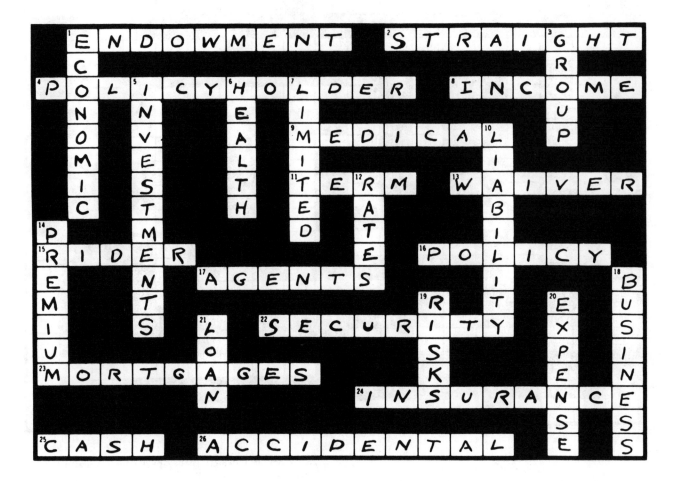

This puzzle was taken from <u>Policies</u> <u>for</u> <u>Protection</u> and is used here through the courtesy of the Institute of Life Insurance.

C. SOURCES OF SUPPLEMENTARY MATERIAL

American Council of Life Insurance
Educational and Community Services
1850 K Street, NW
Washington, DC 20006

Educational Division
Life Insurance Institute
Health Insurance Institute
277 Park Avenue
New York, NY 10017

Insurance Information Institute
Educational Division
110 William Street
New York, NY 10038

D. TRANSPARENCY MASTERS, POSTERS, AND BULLETIN BOARDS

Sketches appear on succeeding pages.

FLOWER OF SECURITY

This poster is made to resemble a flower which when first shown is completely closed. Each day of the week you pull down a petal of the flower which has something pertaining to insurance written on it. Thus when the flower is completely bloomed you have certain facts about insurance showing on the flower. This is also a good way to help your students to arrange questions in their minds to ask you during the teaching of this unit.

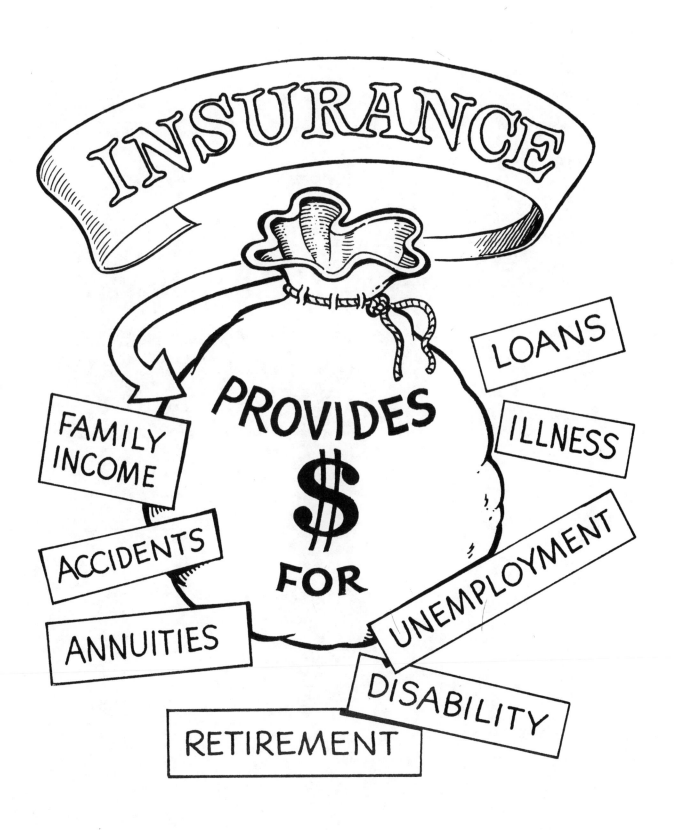

HOMEOWNERS INSURANCE

COVERS THESE RISKS

HAIL & WINDSTORM

VEHICLE DAMAGE

FIRE & LIGHTNING

VANDALISM RIOT & COMMOTION

FALLING OBJECTS

EXPLOSION

BURGLARY & THEFT

SMOKE

THE EFFECTIVE USE OF CREDIT

A. FOREWORD

Credit is a means of obtaining something of value in exchange for a promise to pay for it at some future time. It is a unique feature of our business system; a tool that helps our economic system work effectively. It provides purchasing power when it can be used to the advantage of both the seller and the consumer.

At some time during nearly everyone's lifetime, he will use some form of credit. Therefore, it is important for people to know what credit is, and when and how to use it. It is important to know how it affects the lives of individuals, business, and the national economy.

For most consumers, credit is a convenient method of paying for certain purchases. Others use credit to meet unexpected or extraordinary demands for cash, while still others use it to make instalment purchases.

Billions of dollars' worth of goods and services are sold on credit annually. Because of credit's widespread use, students should learn about its different forms, where credit may be obtained, the cost of credit, and how to manage credit transactions properly.

B. SUGGESTIONS FOR LAUNCHING THE TOPIC

1. This topic may be introduced by displaying before the class members a good camera or a portable radio and giving them its cash price. Ask them how much more they would be willing to pay in order to be able to use it now but have the privilege of spreading payments over nine months. Find the average amount they are willing to pay, then give them the instalment price. If the cost of buying on instalments is more than the average amount they

were willing to pay, open the matter for discussion and see if they would pay the instalment price.

2. Have students state the reasons why they would want to buy on credit, and ask them to name some places where they can buy on credit.

3. Hand out a case problem such as those described on pages 110-111, and have discussion after the students have made their solutions.

4. Collect and display different types of credit contracts, credit cards, and charge plates, etc., on the bulletin board.

5. Dramatic Skit. Here is a brief skit which two students may present as an introduction for the study of credit.

A NEW DRESS

Mother, sitting in living room at desk, looking through a group of bills with a look on her face of, "How will I ever make all these payments?" Daughter wanders in and sits down.

DAUGHTER (Low, pausing between words): Mother . . . Mother . . . hey, Mother . . .

MOTHER (uninterested): What is it?

DAUGHTER: Remember that party I'm going to Saturday night? Well, you know how bad I need a new dress and. . . . Well, I saw one today that would be just perfect! Mother, the saleslady put it back for me and she said you could charge it. Please??!!

MOTHER (holds up bills): I already have so many bills that by the time I make a payment here and a payment there I won't have anything left. If I could only make one payment for all of them I would feel so relieved and . . .

DAUGHTER (excitedly): Say! That's it! I saw an ad in the newspaper for a charge account where you pay once monthly for all bills. Wait, just a minute, and I'll see if I can find it. (Hurries to the wastepaper basket and gets yesterday's paper.) Here it is! Look, it's VISA!

MOTHER: Well, this looks just like what I'm looking for. I will go to the bank first thing in the morning and inquire about it. Maybe you can get that new dress after all.

Follow this by a discussion using, among others, the following questions:

    a. What is the advantage of combining one's bills into one charge account at the bank?

    b. Is there any disadvantage to this?

    c. Does having only one payment to make enable one's money to go further?

    d. How much may a person charge on VISA (or Master Charge)?

    e. How does the cash advance part of VISA work?

    f. What rate of interest does one pay when using VISA?

6. Use an attitude inventory such as on page 274.

What Is Your Opinion About
Buying on Credit?

Directions: Indicate your reaction to each of the following
statements by stating whether you (1) agree,
(2) partially agree, (3) disagree, or (4) are
uncertain. For each statement write one of the
words: agree, partially, disagree, or uncertain
in the appropriate answer space provided.

1. Persons who buy for cash are better financial managers than those who buy on credit. _____

2. Paying cash helps prevent one from buying
unnecessary things. _____

3. The dollar cost to buy on credit is more
important than the percentage rate it costs. _____

4. The use of charge accounts encourages
a person to overbuy. _____

5. Customers who buy on credit should be
charged more than those who pay cash. _____

6. People should not buy on credit, for it
discourages the practice of thrift. _____

7. Credit is largely for the rich and should
be avoided by poor people. _____

8. The advantages of buying on credit outweigh the disadvantages. _____

9. It is better to borrow money to pay for
an expensive item than it is to buy it
on the instalment plan. _____

10. Credit buying of goods lowers a consumer's standard of living. _____

11. Buying on credit should be limited to the
purchase of goods that last a long time. _____

12. Buying goods on credit has an influence
on the amount of goods produced in this
country. _____

13. People who buy goods on credit can own more
goods than if they always pay cash. _____

C. SUGGESTED ACTIVITIES

1. Have the students bring to class newspaper advertisements that offer goods for sale on the instalment plan. Direct their attention to such information as the type of goods offered for sale, the amount of the down payment, the stated rate of interest, service charges, the number of payments, and the total amount to be paid. What information is missing from the ads that would be helpful if it were included?

2. Divide the class into committees and have them find out what kinds of credit plans are used locally, such as lay-away plan, personalized budget plan, credit cards, revolving credit plan, etc. Both the purpose and nature of each plan should be clarified.

3. Have a committee visit local merchants that extend credit to teen-agers and report under what conditions the credit is extended and what it costs. If any students in the class have charge accounts of their own, include them as members of the committee.

4. Invite a banker or a representative of a credit bureau to explain to the class how credit ratings are established and how they are sometimes abused.

5. Have a debate on why consumers should use credit and why they should not.

6. Appoint a committee to make a bulletin board illustrating the three C's of credit.

7. Photograph sufficient copies of an instalment purchase contract so that each two class members may have a copy. Discuss the clauses that pertain to repossession of goods, defaulting on payments, title remaining with the seller until the full purchase price is paid, etc.

8. Have a student committee report on the procedures followed in opening charge accounts in local stores.

9. Appoint a committee to obtain information about bankruptcy procedures in the state. The committee members should find out what procedures are used when filing bankruptcy, to what degree filing frees one from the payment of his debts, its effect on one's future, etc.

10. Show the film, The Wise Use of Credit, which discusses the basic principles of using credit, criteria for determining how much credit to use, cost factors, and the consumer--the one who is paying for credit service.

11. As a review activity, play the matching game using the terms and definitions on page 277, following the directions on page 185.

12. Appoint a student to report on the details of the small-loan law in your state.

13. Panel Discussion. The "Pros and Cons of Instalment Buying" or "Use and Abuse of Consumer Credit."

14. Student Report. Assign a student to interview a local banker on the advantages of credit and report to the class.

15. Have the students prepare a list of items that are commonly purchased on credit and a list of those that are rarely bought on credit. Why is credit used or not used in each case?

16. Have your students complete an application for credit such as the one on page 278.

17. Use the displays on page 279 for class discussion.

THE MATCHING GAME

1. Revolving credit plan

2. Interest

3. Instalment credit

4. Capacity

5. Repossess

6. Collateral

7. Promissory note

8. True interest

9. Credit rating

10. Bank

20. The customer buys according to a credit limit, makes monthly payments, and is charged interest on the unpaid balance.

18. Amount paid for the use of money

16. A type of credit that provides for repaying the amount owed in two or more payments

19. The ability to pay a debt

15. To take back goods paid on credit if the buyer fails to make payment when due

13. Property used as security for a loan

11. A written promise to repay a loan by a certain time

17. Usually means total percent cost for a year

12. Determined by the way a person has used credit in the past

14. Leading source of consumer loans

ANSWERS

1.	20	6.	13
2.	18	7.	11
3.	16	8.	17
4.	19	9.	12
5.	15	10.	14

CREDIT APPLICATION

PRINT--use ball point pen--all information confidential
Fill out completely

Name		Age	Spouse's First Name	
Address			Spouse's Age	Dependent Children
City-State		Zip	Own Home ☐ Rent ☐ Room ☐ Live with Parents ☐
			How Long	Phone Number
Former Address (if less than three years at present address)				How Long
Previously Applied for Charge Account? Single ☐ Married ☐ Separated ☐ Divorced ☐ Widow(er) ☐ Authorized Buyers				
No ☐ Yes--Where?				
Employer (or Firm if Self-Employed)		Address		
Position	Social Security Number		Salary Monthly	How Long
Former Employer (if less than three years with present employer)		Address		Position	How Long
Spouse's Employer		Position	Salary Monthly	How Long
Other Income Source	Amount-Month $	Bank-Branch	Checking ☐ Saving ☐
Nearest Relative Not at Your Address		Address		Relationship ☐
Credit References-Location-Account Number				

```
┌─────────────────────────────┐
│  ┌───────────────────────┐  │
│  │                       │  │
│  │                       │  │
│  │       ACTUAL          │  │        or a facsimile
│  │    CREDIT CARD        │  │
│  │                       │  │
│  │                       │  │
│  └───────────────────────┘  │
└─────────────────────────────┘
```

Explain to the class that the owner of the card displayed
may purchase goods by merely signing his name.

Ask: What does it take to get one of these? Write student
responses on the chalkboard.

Show a picture of a person dreaming of buying a car.

If George does not have the cash to pay for this car, how
may he establish his credit rating in order to buy it?

a. Good reputation -------------- Character
b. Home ownership --------------- Capital
c. Earning power --------------- Capacity
d. Pledge other valuables
   for a loan ------------------- Collateral

D. SOURCES OF SUPPLEMENTARY MATERIAL

CUNA International, Inc.
1617 Sherman Avenue
P.O. Box 431
Madison, WI 53701

Educational Services Division
National Consumer Finance Association
1000 Sixteenth Street, NW
Washington, DC 20036

Household Finance Corporation
Prudential Plaza
Chicago, IL 60601

The Kiplinger Washington Editors, Inc.
Editors Park, MD 20782

National Credit Union Administration
Washington, DC 20456

E. TRANSPARENCY MASTERS, POSTERS, AND BULLETIN BOARDS

Sketches appear on succeeding pages.

WHY DO CONSUMERS USE CREDIT?

1. Credit is convenient.
2. Credit gives immediate use of goods.
3. Credit can help one save money.
4. Credit can improve one's standard of living.
5. Credit customers may receive better service.
6. Wise use of credit establishes a credit rating.

Show students a poster on credit and ask the question: Where do you think would be the best place to borrow money? When they begin to discuss the question and try to answer where and why, lead them into the study of each loan agency.

CREDIT

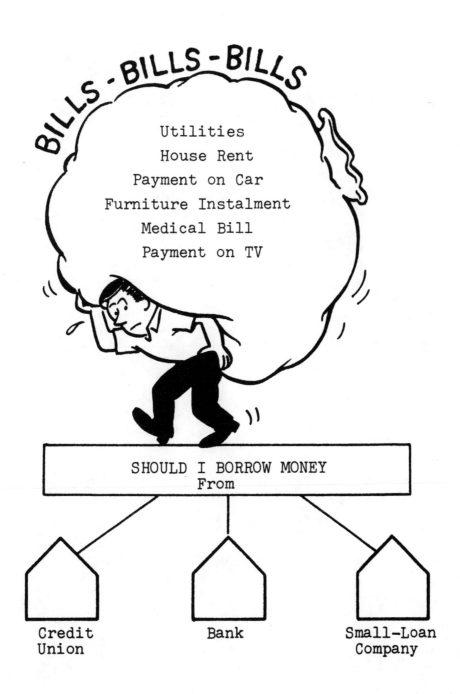

WHAT DETERMINES Your CREDIT RATING ?

CHARACTER . . . . .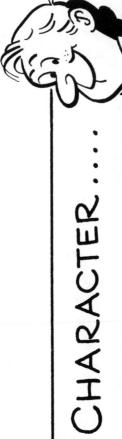

CAPACITY . . . . . .

CAPITAL . . . . . .

GOVERNMENT, BUSINESS, AND LABOR

A. GUIDE SHEET FOR STUDENT USE IN STUDY OF THE TOPIC

When you have completed your study of this topic you should know or be able to do these things:

1. Describe the ways that government serves business and the people.

2. Understand some of the ways government aids agriculture and business through loans, subsidies, etc.

3. Know how the government functions as a producer--the types of business services that are provided by government.

4. Understand why the services of government are not free.

5. Explain how the costs of government are met by taxes.

6. Recognize that taxes rise because of increased government spending, which is caused by increasing public needs and wants.

7. Identify the various taxes which comprise our tax system and explain the characteristics of each.

8. List and explain the characteristics of a good tax.

9. Identify the sources and approximate percentages of state, local, and federal revenues.

10. Define and identify progressive, proportional, and regressive taxes.

11. Explain how taxes can be used to produce economic changes.

12. Explain the term "deficit spending."

13. Complete correctly simple federal and state income tax returns.

14. Explain the role of labor in our business system and its contributions to the effective functioning of the system.

15. Know how, why, and when labor unions started and what has helped them grow.

16. Explain what organized labor expects from business management.

17. Understand how union officers serve their rank-and-file members and how unions help workers.

18. Explain the types of bargaining and political activity in which union members engage.

B. SUGGESTIONS FOR LAUNCHING THE TOPIC

1. Show slides or pictures that illustrate the different
types of business services that governments provide, such as
schools, fire protection, health inspections, police, library,
streets, parking, and bus service. As each illustration is shown,
have the students identify the service and prepare a master list
of services. (An alternate way of achieving this same end is to
illustrate only two or three services and ask the students to
report on other services the next day.)

2. Invite some person from the county courthouse (or mayor's
office) to speak on the topic, "The Role of Government in Business."

3. Start by describing very briefly the various functions
of government as they relate to the business community, such as
licensing, subsidizing, regulation, production of business services, etc. Ask the class members how these would be performed if
government did not perform them, and what the relative advantages
and disadvantages are of having the government do them. For
example, how else could safety, as provided by the police department, be achieved if it were not provided by the government?

4. Start with the preparation of a simple state or federal
income tax form. Then raise the question as to why taxes are paid
to the government and what services are rendered by the government to individuals and to businesses.

5. Give each class member a 3 x 5 inch card or a small sheet
of paper and ask each one to draw a line down the middle of it.
On the left side, have the students list all the services of
government they receive and on the right side have them list all
the types of taxes they pay. (Discuss the compiled results and
keep for reference purposes at the end of the study of the topic.
The activity may be repeated by using the reverse side of the
card or paper.)

6. Use the following attitude inventory:

What Is Your Opinion About Government, Business, and Labor?

Directions: Indicate your reaction to each of the following statements by stating whether you (1) agree, (2) partially agree, (3) disagree, or (4) are uncertain. For each statement write one of the words: agree, partially, disagree, or uncertain in the appropriate answer space provided.

1. The government should stay out of business and let private enterprise operate according to the law of supply and demand (free of government interference). _____

2. Labor should be considered a cost of production and like other costs kept to a minimum. _____

3. Only those persons who are financially able should pay taxes to support the government. _____

4. Strikes should be prohibited by law and differences between labor and management settled by compulsory arbitration. _____

5. Labor should be considered as a partner in production and should share in the fruits of production (profits). _____

6. Business should operate according to the rules of fair play but should police itself rather than be regulated by the government. _____

7. Government services come to the public as free services. _____

8. Persons who work for the government should not have the right to strike. _____

9. Large labor unions are so powerful they should be subject to the same anti-monopoly laws that regulate large businesses. _____

10. There are some business services that can best be rendered by the government rather than by private enterprise. _____

11. Everybody loses when labor goes out on strike: business, labor, government, and the public. _____

C. SUGGESTED ACTIVITIES

1. Have a committee of two or three students interview a leading local labor leader and report to the class on "The Role of Labor in Our Business and Political Life."

2. Invite a plant manager or factory foreman to speak to the class on "Labor-Management Relations."

3. Have a committee report to the class on "What We Receive for Our Tax Dollars."

4. Have a student panel discuss "Government Services Are Not Free!"

5. Have a student committee interview the local tax assessor and report to the class on how property is assessed, and how tax rates are determined and collected.

6. As a class project make a special study of various taxes (sales, property, income, excise, etc.) from the point of view of whether and how they may be passed on to someone else.

7. Prepare personal income tax returns, both federal and state.

8. Have a student interview the executive secretary of a local union and report to the class on: "How Nonunion Workers Benefit from the Presence of Labor Unions in Local Industry."

9. Have a student use supplementary booklets and current periodical references and report to the class on "What Organized Labor Expects from Management."

10. Have some person from the local post office talk to the class on "How to Use the Postal Service Effectively" or "How the U.S. Postal Service Serves Business."

11. Have each student watch the local papers and current issues of the magazines received in their homes for a period of two weeks for articles dealing with government, business, and labor. As they are brought to class exhibit them on the tack board with each article mounted on a piece of colored paper along with the person's name who brought it.

12. Many union contracts have escalator clauses that provide for wage adjustments as the cost of living changes. Have the students ask their parents why or why not workers' wages should be related to changes in the Consumer Price Index.

13. An interesting review activity covering taxes would be to use the word puzzle on page 296. The solution is on page 297.

14. Introduce a discussion of taxes by using the suggestion on page 298.

15. Have some student use the standard reference books in the library and determine what percentage of all gainfully employed persons work for the government.

16. Have a committee investigate the topic "What Organizations and Institutions in Our Community Are Exempt from Paying Taxes" and discuss whether they think this is a justifiable practice.

17. As a teacher activity you should explain that the "characteristics of a good tax" apply to the total tax package and that no individual type of tax can meet all these criteria. Also, since most persons are overexposed to the philosophy that "nothing is sure but death and taxes" you should see that the positive side of services being rendered by the government is brought out.

18. As a class project, try to determine what groups of persons in the local community receive payments from the government (the usual government employees, firemen, policemen, teachers, highway department workers, welfare recipients, social security beneficiaries, etc.).

19. Have a class discussion on taxes and ask the students to solve the puzzle on page 299. The solution is on page 300.

THE WORD PUZZLE

Look for words that represent kinds of taxes, sources of tax income, or criteria of a good tax. Circle all words that seem to qualify. The words may be spelled from left to right or top to bottom.

S	A	L	E	S	O	O	J	X	I
D	A	B	I	L	I	T	Y	Z	N
P	D	R	A	C	N	T	S	A	H
R	G	A	T	C	C	S	E	B	E
O	Q	N	A	H	O	P	E	O	R
P	T	R	R	A	M	W	S	O	I
E	X	C	I	S	E	Z	T	Q	T
R	K	C	F	S	I	J	A	I	A
T	H	E	F	V	T	W	T	B	N
Y	T	C	H	T	L	A	E	W	C
R	E	G	R	E	S	S	I	V	E

S	A	L	E	S	O	O	J	X	I
D	A	B	I	L	I	T	Y	Z	N
P	D	R	A	C	N	T	S	A	H
R	G	A	T	C	C	S	E	B	E
O	Q	N	A	H	O	P	E	O	R
P	T	R	R	A	M	W	S	O	I
E	X	C	I	S	E	Z	T	Q	T
R	K	C	F	S	I	J	A	I	A
T	H	E	F	V	T	W	T	B	N
Y	T	C	H	T	L	A	E	W	C
R	E	G	R	E	S	S	I	V	E

297

Cut each of the letters out of colored construction paper or cardboard, about 14 inches high. Ask the students what kind of taxes they pay. As they give you a particular kind of tax, place the letter on which that tax is written in its appropriate place and discuss the tax briefly, just enough to introduce it for further study. In all probability they will not name the taxes in the correct order but place them up in the order they name them.

The letter <u>A</u> may be the last one given--you might even have to supply it yourself.

(A tackboard may be used instead of the flannel board.)

What Kind of Taxes Do You Pay?

THE CROSSWORD PUZZLE

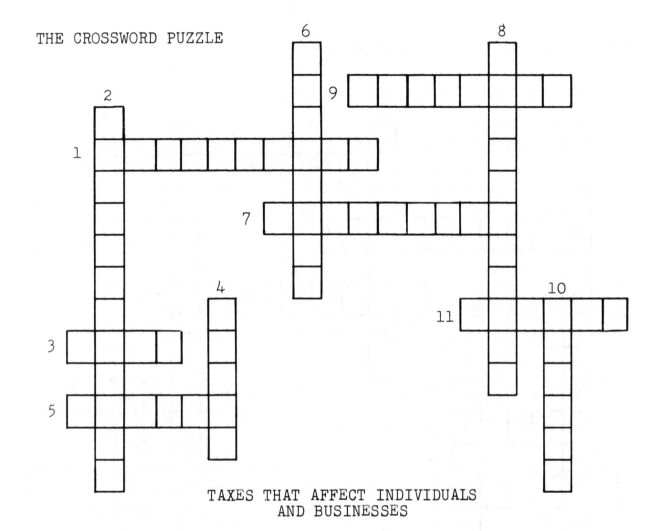

TAXES THAT AFFECT INDIVIDUALS
AND BUSINESSES

ACROSS

1. A tax for which the burden increases as ability to pay decreases.

3. A tax on property or money which is given to other persons.

5. A tax on one's earnings.

7. A tax assessed against the value of a natural resource removed from the earth.

9. A tax on real estate or personal items such as automobiles or household goods.

11. A tax that can not be shifted to someone else.

DOWN

2. A tax where the rate is the same regardless of the amount involved.

4. A tax levied on the purchases of most goods.

6. A tax that can be shifted to someone else.

8. A tax where the rate increases as the amount taxed increases.

10. A sales tax levied on a specific product or service.

Solution

D. SOURCES OF SUPPLEMENTARY MATERIAL

AFL-CIO
815 Sixteenth Street, NW
Washington, DC 20006

Automobile Manufacturing Association, Inc.
Educational Services
320 New Center Building
Detroit, MI 48202

Chamber of Commerce of the United States
1615 H Street, NW
Washington, DC 20062

Dun and Bradstreet Inc.
99 Church Street
New York, NY 10007

International Labor Office
Public Information Department
Washington Branch
666 Eleventh Street, NW
Washington, DC 20001

Joint Council on Economic Education
1212 Park Avenue
New York, NY 10036

National Right to Work Committee
8316 Arlington Boulevard
Fairfax, VA 22038

Tax Foundation, Inc.
50 Rockefeller Plaza
New York, NY 10020

U.S. Department of Commerce
Social and Economic Statistics Administration
Washington, DC 20233

U.S. Department of Labor
Bureau of Labor Statistics
Washington, DC 20212

U.S. Government Printing Office
Superintendent of Documents
Washington, DC 20402

E. TRANSPARENCY MASTERS, POSTERS, AND BULLETIN BOARDS

Sketches appear on succeeding pages.

GOVERNMENT IS INVOLVED IN BUSINESS

REGULATES RATES OF UTILITIES & TRANSPORTATION COMPANIES

BUYS GOODS PRODUCED BY OTHERS

PROVIDES CERTAIN TYPES OF SERVICES

ASSURES COMPETITION & PREVENTS MONOPOLIES

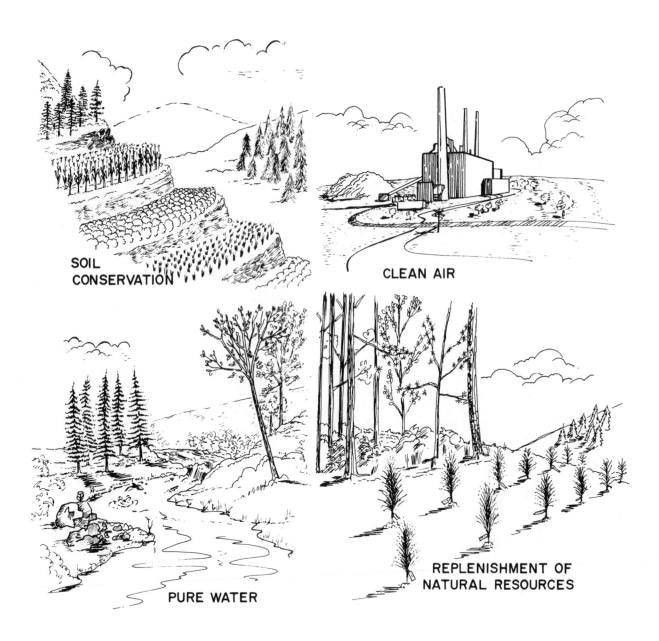

SOIL
CONSERVATION

CLEAN AIR

PURE WATER

REPLENISHMENT OF
NATURAL RESOURCES

WHAT ORGANIZED LABOR WANTS

A LIVING WAGE

SAFE AND CLEAN
WORKING CONDITIONS

A SOUND PENSION
SYSTEM

CONTRACTUAL
AGREEMENTS

CONSIDERATION OF
COMPLAINTS

TWO-WAY
COMMUNICATION
WITH THE
MANAGERS

SOURCES OF GOVERNMENT REVENUE

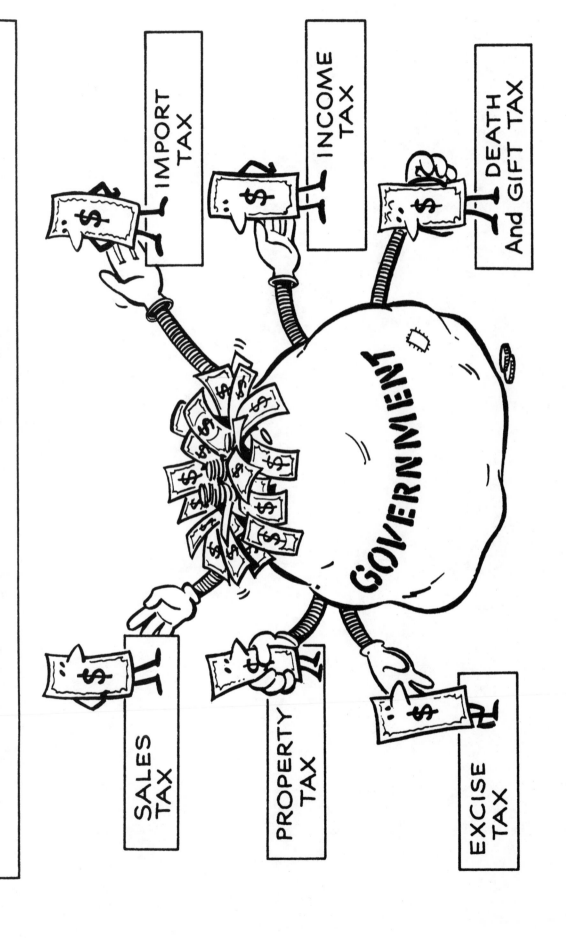

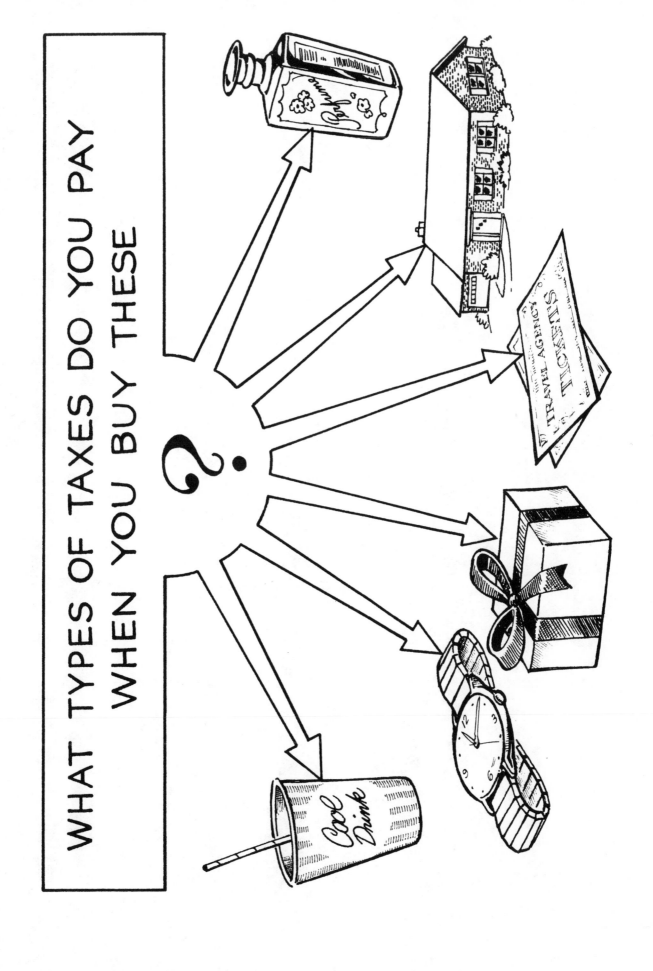

WHAT TYPES OF TAXES DO YOU PAY WHEN YOU BUY THESE

CONTRACTS

A. SUGGESTED ACTIVITIES

1. Have students bring advertisements to class and examine them to see if they meet the requirements of an offer. Discuss the means of acceptance required for each of the items determined to be an offer.

2. Have students bring copies of sales agreements, leases, etc., to class and discuss the features of each.

3. Have students watch the news media for reports on charges of contract fraud.

4. Have an attorney meet with your class to discuss how to read and understand a contract.

5. Contact the small claims court clerk to find out when a local case involving breach of contract is to be heard. Get permission to take your class to court on that day.

6. Ask the small claims court judge to describe to your class some of the cases that have been resolved involving contracts.

7. Divide the students into groups. Ask each group to develop laws which will govern the sale of some product such as corn or toys. Compare their laws and relate them to the necessity of a Uniform Commercial Code for interstate commerce.

8. Discuss the advantages and disadvantages of prenuptial (marriage) contracts.

9. Use case studies such as those in the next section for discussion.

THE WORD PUZZLE

Look for words that are associated with contracts. The words may be spelled from left to right or top to bottom.

M	A	L	N	O	R	E	V	O	C	A	T	I	O	N
E	N	T	R	L	E	M	S	V	O	L	A	P	F	E
A	D	U	R	E	S	S	T	A	U	B	C	W	F	Y
D	H	N	O	K	B	O	A	G	N	E	L	T	E	R
O	L	A	G	E	N	C	Y	R	T	I	R	E	R	T
T	E	C	H	A	O	B	R	E	E	M	A	L	E	L
F	A	C	O	N	S	I	D	E	R	A	T	I	O	N
B	R	E	A	C	H	L	O	M	O	R	I	N	T	S
E	A	P	L	T	O	A	S	E	F	I	F	T	O	N
R	E	T	H	E	L	T	E	N	F	V	Y	E	S	T
F	R	A	U	D	T	E	R	T	E	A	S	N	E	O
A	T	N	S	O	L	R	A	R	R	L	E	T	I	F
N	A	C	T	I	C	A	P	A	C	I	T	Y	R	E
O	P	E	R	E	O	L	A	N	E	D	I	S	E	N
L	U	R	V	N	N	E	R	D	L	E	N	E	W	T

```
M  A  L  N  O  R  E  V  O  C  A  T  I  O  N
E  N  T  R  L  E  M  S  V  O  L  A  P  F  E
A  D  U  R  E  S  S  T  A  U  B  C  W  F  Y
D  H  N  O  K  B  O  A  G  N  E  L  T  E  R
O  L  A  G  E  N  C  Y  R  T  I  R  E  R  T
T  E  C  H  A  O  B  R  E  M  A  L  E  L  L
F  A  C  O  N  S  I  D  E  R  A  T  I  O  N
B  R  E  A  C  H  L  O  M  O  R  I  N  T  S
E  A  P  L  T  O  A  S  E  F  I  F  T  O  N
R  E  T  H  E  L  T  E  N  F  V  Y  E  S  T
F  R  A  U  D  T  E  R  T  E  A  S  N  E  O
A  T  N  S  O  L  R  A  R  R  L  E  T  I  F
N  A  C  T  I  C  A  P  A  C  I  T  Y  R  E
O  P  E  R  E  O  L  A  N  E  D  I  S  E  N
L  U  R  V  N  N  E  R  D  L  E  N  E  W  T
```

B. CASE STUDIES

A Lease

After graduation from college, Mike and Doug decided to move away from home and share an apartment. They found an apartment, made a deposit, and signed a lease for one year. After living in the apartment three months, they decided that they would rather live at home again. Their landlord told them that if they left the apartment, they would have to forfeit their deposit and continue paying the rent until new tenants could be found for the apartment. Mike and Doug thought that one-month's notice was the only consideration they needed to give the landlord. What do you think is fair in a situation such as this?

Door-to-Door Sales

While in college, Mona was visited by a salesman who convinced her that she needed a variety of cooking utensils. She filled out a form ordering the utensils, made a down payment, and agreed to pay the balance over a six-month period. Three weeks later, she decided that she didn't want the cookware, but the company refused to accept the return of the utensils. The company also informed Mona that the balance due had to be paid. Mona feels that the company should take back the cookware because it was never used. What arguments can you give to support Mona's view? The cookware company's view?

Employment Finder's Fee

Samantha had been unable to find a job, but a friend told her about an employment agency in town. The employment agency officer had Samantha sign an agreement which required the payment of a $300 fee if Samantha accepted a position which they located for her. The agency found Samantha a job, but after only three weeks, Samantha decided she didn't like the job and quit. The employment agency demanded that she pay the $300 fee even though she was out of work. Samantha felt that since the agency sent her to a job she didn't like, it was not her fault that it did not work out. Therefore, she felt she did not owe the agency until they found her a job that she liked. What do you think?

Unordered Merchandise

(Example A)

Mr. and Mrs. Smith bought a house. The previous owners had been receiving milk deliveries, and they left the delivery box on the front porch. The milk company had not learned of the change of home ownership and the usual delivery was made. Mr. and Mrs. Smith consumed the products which were delivered. Must they pay for them? Why or why not?

(Example B)

Bob opened his mailbox one day to find a necktie in a box addressed to him from a company which he had never patronized. Even though he had not ordered the tie, a bill for the cost of the tie was enclosed. Was an offer made? Did opening the box legally obligate Bob to pay for the tie? If Bob wears the tie, will he be legally required to pay for it?

Advertising Error

A sale advertisement for a television set was misprinted in a newspaper. Instead of reading $549.95, it read $49.95. Bill Jones demanded that the store honor its offer by accepting his $49.95. Must the store do so? Why or why not?

C. SOURCES OF SUPPLEMENTARY MATERIALS

>   Federal Trade Commission
>   6th Street and Pennsylvania Avenue, NW
>   Washington, DC   20580
>
>   Legal Services Corporation
>   733 15th Street, NW
>   Washington, DC   20005
>
>   US Postal Inspection Service
>   475 L'Enfant Plaza, SW
>   Washington, DC   20260
>
>   Your State Attorney General's Office

D. TRANSPARENCY MASTERS, POSTERS, AND BULLETIN BOARDS

Sketches appear on succeeding pages.

IS THIS A CONTRACT?

ESSENTIALS OF A CONTRACT

1. Competent Parties
2. Mutual Assent
3. Legal Purpose
4. Consideration
5. Required Form

CONSIDERATION

"I WILL GLADLY PAY YOU $500.00 FOR YOUR STEREO."

BENEFIT: Receipt of $500.00
DETRIMENT: Giving up the stereo

BENEFIT: Receipt of the stereo
DETRIMENT: Giving up $500.00

Index

326